Travel with
Children

MAUREEN WHEELER

Travel with Children

3rd edition

Published by
    Lonely Planet Publications
    Head Office: PO Box 617, Hawthorn, Vic 3122, Australia
    Branches: 150 Linden St, Oakland, CA 94607, USA
                    10a Spring Place, London NW5 3BH, UK
                    71 bis rue du Cardinal Lemoine, 75005 Paris, France

Printed by
    The Bookmaker Pty Ltd
    Printed in China

Cover illustration by
Valerie Tellini

First Published
May 1985

This Edition
August 1995

Although the authors and publisher have tried to make the information as accurate as possible, they accept no responsibility for any loss, injury or inconvenience sustained by any person using this book.

National Library of Australia Cataloguing in Publication Data

Wheeler, Maureen
    Travel with Children

    3rd ed.
    Includes index.
    ISBN 0 86442 299 7.

    1. Children - Travel. I. Title. (Series: Lonely Planet travel survival kit).

910.202

Maureen Wheeler

Maureen Wheeler was born in Belfast, Northern Ireland. At age 20 she moved to the 'big city' – London, where three days later she met Tony Wheeler on a park bench in Regent's Park. They were married a year later and set off to see the world, ending up in Australia. In between trips, Maureen completed a degree in social work but faced with a choice between a career and travelling, chose to make travel her career. The birth of Tashi and then Kieran meant that travel with children became a way of life for the Wheelers. Teenage Tashi and Kieran still accompany Maureen and Tony on their frequent travels and considerably enliven the experience.

This Book

For many people of my generation travel as children was most likely to be a visit to grandma, or a week or two at a not too distant beach. Few children travelled 'abroad' with their parents (actually comparatively few parents travelled abroad). Nowadays that has changed considerably; many of the people who are now parents spent a lot of time travelling in the '60s, '70s and '80s, exploring places that to their parents were only names in a song or movie. The trails across Asia, Africa and South America which were once peopled by young, curious Westerners are tramped by the same people, just older and wiser (?). The trips are shorter due to the waiting jobs, but the curiosity is still strong, and more and more often these travellers are accompanied by their young children.

Tony, Maureen, Kieran & Tashi Wheeler – Outback Australia, 1993

The first edition of this book was a result of having been asked for information many times by parents wondering if travel had to be postponed until the children were older, or if it was possible when they were young. For Tony and me, travel is our business and an integral part of our lives, so the question of 'whether' did not arise, just the question of 'how'. The second edition saw the introduction of personal accounts from other families of experiences they've had on the road. This third edition has been expanded and updated and includes travel stories from LP authors, LP staff and LP readers who have travelled with their kids. For the first time Tashi and Kieran have their say on travel with parents: both have been travelling the world since they were babies.

Maureen Wheeler

From the Publisher

This book was coordinated by Hugh Finlay and edited by Kate Cody. The proofreader was Steve Womersley and the artwork check was completed by Mary Neighbour. Vicki Beale designed the book and Rachel Black was responsible for layout. Valerie Tellini was responsible for the cover illustration and cover design, chapter and travel tips icons while Margaret Jung illustrated the travel stories. Sharon Wertheim did the indexing.

Thanks also to Tony & Maureen Wheeler, James & Pauline Lyon, Hugh Finlay and Linda Henderson, Peter & Lorraine Turner, Andrew Draffen & Stella Alves da Motta Draffen, María Massolo and Wayne Bernhardson, Susan Forsyth and John Noble, Kate Cody and Ben Taylor, and Julie Young for the use of their family holiday photos.

Warning & Request

Because every family is different, your experiences of travel with children will vary from ours. So if you find things better or worse than we suggested, please write and tell us and help make the next edition better!

Your letters will be used to help update future editions and, where possible, important changes will also be included in a Stop Press section in reprints.

We greatly appreciate all information that is sent to us by travellers and particularly from travelling families with their hectic schedules. Back at Lonely Planet we employ a hard-working readers' letters team to sort through the many letters we receive. The best ones will be rewarded with a free copy of the next edition or another Lonely Planet guide if you prefer.

CONTENTS

TRAVEL WITH CHILDREN

Tony and I have travelled ever since we first met in the early '70s. Although at times families and friends have worried about our choice of destination, or method of getting there, most people seemed to agree that travel was beneficial and we were very lucky to do so much. Knowing how much travel was a part of our lives, not to mention our livelihood, they were quite surprised when we added children to the equation, deeming it quite impossible to continue travelling in the areas we did with children.

When Tashi was six months old, we went on a trip around Malaysia, Singapore, England, Ireland, the USA and back to Australia. We travelled for five months and discovered that it was a totally new experience with a child. Two years later her brother Kieran joined us and he took his first real trip, to the island of Bali, when he was four months old. Before his first birthday he had also been to Thailand, Nepal, India and Sri Lanka.

Our children are now 14 and 12-years-old and together we have made trips to: Canada and the USA in North America; to Mexico and several of the Andean countries in Latin America; to a number of Pacific Islands; to New Zealand and Australia (of course); to Japan, Hong Kong and Macau in North-East Asia; to Indonesia, Singapore, Malaysia and Thailand in South-East Asia; to Nepal, India and Sri Lanka on the Indian subcontinent; to Kenya and Zimbabwe in Africa; to England and Ireland in Britain; and to the Caribbean, Egypt, Jordan, Israel, France, Italy and Switzerland.

So travel with children is possible, but is it worth it? Well, if travelling is one of your major pleasures in life, why stop? Children can increase travel hassles, but they can also make it even more fun.

Tony and I have taken Tashi and Kieran to places we had visited before, and have found that it is a new experience with them in tow. We meet more local people: parenthood is universal so we immediately have something in common with most people we meet. The experience is fascinating for us and the children enjoy it and benefit immensely from meeting other people and their children.

The problems exist of course. How you travel and where you stay and eat all have to be considered more carefully when you have children with you, and more care has to be taken to ensure the children stay healthy. It can be tiring: there will be times when you feel hot, dusty and fed up after a long trip, or you may have had a particularly hassling day and you badly need some peace and quiet, and then there's junior also hassled, also fed up and you're supposed to do something. At times you wish you had listened to all the advice and stayed home; this book is for all the dedicated travellers who feel that to stay home, or to limit travel to the safest, easiest options 'because of the children' is to deny yourself and your children the most fantastic adventure you can have.

GETTING READY

PLANNING
Children's Ages

The age of your children is an important factor to consider before you travel.

Babies Babies require a lot of equipment – nappies, changes of clothes, special implements – and some kind of routine for naps, feeding and changing. They may also get you up at night; in a hotel that may not go down too well with neighbours. There is also more anxiety with babies on the move: they can't tell you if they are too hot, too cold, or get a stomach ache. As parents are at their most anxious with small babies, travelling probably exacerbates that anxiety. On the plus side, babies are portable and easy to entertain – a day in a museum is a possibility with a baby in a backpack or stroller. This is probably the only stage of a child's life you get to dictate where you go and what you do!

Toddlers Toddlers are probably the most difficult; all that energy and trying-to-do-everything and all the frustrations of not being allowed to. You need to be extremely watchful as they are inclined to pick up unsavoury objects, pat the local mangy dog, cuddle the fleabag cat, or wander off when their eye is caught by something intriguing. Also, toddlers are fussy eaters and obstinate in their likes and dislikes. The plus side is the interest toddlers bring to everything.

Older Children From about the age of four on, travel with children becomes a real pleasure. It is still hard work, but also very rewarding as your children now form their own impressions and relationships, and can tell you what they are experiencing. As your children get older they will tell you what they enjoy, and planning trips will be more of a group effort with their likes and dislikes being taken into account, within reason (how many times can you visit Disneyland after all?).

Teenagers Teenagers are almost another book. They will tell you where they will and won't go, and may even draw up contracts negotiating how many 'temple' days and 'ruins' days are a reasonable 'quid pro quo' for beach days or shopping days.

Preparing to Travel

There are lots of ways you can help prepare your children for the trip in the weeks before you leave. Include your children in your planning: ask what they want to bring and let them select the books they would like to have with them. I usually buy a few new books which I produce when we are packing.

As soon as our children were able to walk, they were given their own daypacks to take on the plane with them. In it they carry their books and a few toys; I usually try to have a few surprise books and games for them to find on the plane. You do have to make it clear that it is their daypack and they must carry it (when possible!), so keep it light.

Books A month or so before you depart it is a good idea to get as much literature as you can on the area you are going to. Get tourist literature, books from the library – anything with pictures. Try to find books of legends or children's stories from the region.

Tashi first encountered the Hindu story of Rama and Sita from the *Ramayana* in Bali, loved the story and was enthralled to see pictures depicting the story carved on temple walls, or danced at local festivals. Allusions to it pop up all over South-East Asia and the Indian subcontinent.

For a month to six weeks before we leave home, we read stories about the places we are going to. Even a travel brochure can be made into a story by explaining the pictures. You may be surprised at how much sticks. In Nepal Tashi pointed out women carrying things on their heads: she was delighted to find that many things she saw were 'just like in the book'.

Film Movies on the places you are going to are great. Many films are shot in exotic locations. The Bertolucci movie *Little Buddha* is a great introduction to Nepal and Buddhism.

Restaurants & Outings You can take your children out to eat in restaurants, go for trips, take them for walks – in short prepare them for travelling. Introduce a few different foods or flavours into your cooking. Although most children will recoil on principle when anything new is offered, they will sometimes try new food in a new country when it is served up in a restaurant.

DOCUMENTS
Passports

In most countries a parent can have children added to their own passport. The fee for this, if there is one, will be less than for getting separate passports for the children, but the drawback is that they can only travel with the parent whose passport they appear on. If the children are in the mother's passport they must accompany her if she has to return home for some reason. With very small children that would probably happen anyway, but when they are older it may be a nuisance; and if the father wanted to take them somewhere he couldn't without the mother.

Getting separate passports for your children, while an additional expense, avoids these problems. On the other hand, the passport photograph could show a bald, toothless baby which may not please a five-year-old. To change the photo means more bureaucracy and money. Separate passports also mean that you have that little bit more to carry and take care of (passports are often targeted by thieves).

Tony and I opted for the children going on my passport at first, but now they have passports of their own.

Visas

Children with their own passports require visas just like adults and there don't seem to be any reduced rates. However, if the children are included on the parent's passport, a visa is often only required for the parent, and in some places (such as India or Nepal) this can result in a considerable saving.

Other Documents

Check with your travel agent or the appropriate embassy whether any special documents are required for the country you are travelling to. In Mexico, for example, authorities may require a notarised letter of consent *signed by both parents* permitting a minor (a person under 18-years-old) to enter the country if travelling alone or with one parent. This rule is a direct result of the number of North American parents who run away to Mexico with their children in order to escape custody battles, however it applies to travellers of all nationalities.

COSTS

More is best – it has long been recognised that two cannot live as cheaply as one and you soon realise that taking the kids is not as easy or as cheap as it may have seemed when the children were theoretical rather than actual.

Places to Stay

You can still travel cheaply, and in many places cheaper hotels can be more fun to stay in than the multi-storey, Western-style, 'behave yourself, people are watching' type.

If, however, you are travelling on a shoestring you need to be prepared to upgrade how you travel and where you eat. Concrete floors may be fine, but if you have a child who is crawling you may suddenly realise that the concrete floor, besides being hard, is not always that clean. Or if your child is toddling, shakily, and there is no lock on the toilet door, and the toilet is just a hole in the floor, the stress of watching every moment may not be worth the money you're saving.

Other hassles of very cheap hotels may be the impossibility of keeping out mosquitoes. The rooms may be poorly soundproofed and every noise is audible, including your child lustily bellowing for a drink at 2 am. The bathroom may not have a bath or shower or sink, so washing your children may be a little difficult. Somehow cleanliness becomes more important when you are travelling with children.

Often what was acceptable to you alone is no longer so for your children. You may find that you feel more comfortable in more expensive hotels when you are travelling with children, although you won't necessarily have to spend very much more to find places that are ideal for you and your children.

You can still find places which are both comfortable and cheap in many countries in Asia, Africa and Latin America. We've stayed in superb places which were also very economical, in places as diverse as Mexico, Indonesia, Kenya, Nepal and Peru.

Travelling with young children means that your days start early and usually end early when you have to feed them and get them to bed. So it's nice sometimes to stay in a flashier place which has little bungalows or rooms set around or near the dining area. You can feed the children early, get them to sleep and then go and eat, taking turns to go back to the rooms, say, every 10 minutes to check they are still asleep.

Older children can usually stay up later and accompany you to dinner, but there are occasions when they are tired or you feel like having a more adult dinner. If the restaurant is in the hotel or very close by (and it's a small hotel) you could leave the children drawing or reading and ask somebody to keep an eye on them and call you if necessary. Write down where you will be and make sure your children know exactly where you are.

Places to Eat

Upgrading your eating places is also a good idea. In many places you will find local eating stalls or restaurants that are safe, appetising and cheap but there will also be times when all that is available is an expensive hotel or restaurant, either because other places look too unsavoury, what is on offer simply doesn't appeal to young tastes or because there is simply nothing else. While you may be prepared to eat what is available, snack on fruit or nuts or even just go without a meal, your children may not.

Apart from the health or convenience factors, there will definitely be times when all your children want are a hamburger, French fries and a cold milkshake. Most big hotels can provide a suitable copy almost anywhere in the world and the indulgence is probably worthwhile for the pleasure it will

bring. Children have no real concept of time, so a few weeks is a very long time. To tell your children to wait until they get home in a few weeks for familiar food, is like saying in January that 'next Christmas you'll get to decorate the tree'. Children can feel that they are never going to see home or anything familiar again. The kind of meal that they recognise can help them feel a little more secure, and also reassure them that they won't have to eat 'strange food' for ever.

Room Service Room service should not be overlooked either. Having dinner in your room when you are all tired and can't face the hassle of going to a restaurant is cheap at the price. Likewise, a leisurely breakfast in your room after a week spent getting up and dashing out to see and do things, is also a luxury worth enjoying.

Transport

With small children long bus or train trips are unlikely to be much fun. Being willing to spend more money is useful for those occasions when a flight will get you from A to B in a fraction of the time.

Look for easy ways out: in many countries there are long-distance taxis which can cut hours off a trip, will stop when you want and aren't so crowded – all great advantages when travelling with children. Travelling at a slower pace, staying longer in one place or breaking up a longer trip into separate smaller sections are all ways of breaking the monotony for kids.

TRAVEL TIPS...

The first rule of thumb is to take as little as possible. Keep paring it down to where you think it isn't nearly enough – it almost always is.

WHAT TO BRING

I won't attempt to make a comprehensive list of everything you should bring. However, I will try to catalogue the things that I have found made life a bit easier either for me or the kids.

The first rule of thumb is to take as little as possible. Keep paring it down to where you think it isn't nearly enough – it almost always is. Remember, in general babies' needs are pretty simple and wherever you go people have babies, so you can usually improvise.

Clothes

Cotton is the only material that can be worn comfortably in the tropics. Children really don't need too many clothes, nor clothes that are too fancy – shorts and T-shirts are ideal. For babies a T-shirt and nappy are enough to get around in. A warm sweater and a waterproof jacket or all-in-one-suit should cover most contingencies. These are the tropical basics; what you feel you must have is up to you. Underwear should also be cotton and make sure pants don't rub around the top of the legs, because when the child gets sweaty tight leg bands can cause a rash or fungal infection. A medicated powder or baby powder is also useful on areas that get sweaty.

Although your children will probably want to run around barefoot they should wear light sandals, thongs, or some such protection. There are various worm infections which enter through the skin of the feet and it is a good idea to insist that your children wear something on their feet at all times. Beaches, paths, pavements, tracks, in fact almost the entire surface of some developing countries, will be dotted with animal and human faeces, parasites and bacteria.

In many countries it is also advisable to wear some sort of footwear when paddling in the sea or wading through rock pools, to protect against sharp coral or shells and any creatures that may be lurking. There are many suitable shoes (plastic, open sandals, thongs or light canvas shoes) available.

Nappies

Let me now break the bad news. Nappies, diapers, call them what you will, are non-existent in many developing countries. So is nappy rash. In general, when babies are very small they have old cloths underneath them when they are lying down, and these are changed when necessary. When they are carried cloths are sort of packed under them, not really fastened, just placed strategically. Once on a long bus trip in

India a woman beside me had a very tiny, new baby on her knee; she had the cloth arrangement and also managed to cup her hands under the child at appropriate moments and scoop the collected urine out the window!

At a few months they often wear cotton pants, and when dampness or anything else seeps through, the person carrying the baby holds them out over a gutter or field or wherever and then changes the pants. When they are old enough to toddle they go bare-arsed until they are toilet-trained. When they get the urge they just go wherever they may be. None of which is very helpful to us travelling Westerners.

Your child can probably do without nappies quite a lot of the time. If you spend a while on the beaches, or stay at any one place for a while, no one will mind if they do like the locals. However at night, when travelling, or when shopping, some protection will be necessary. And I'm afraid there is no really easy way.

Getting your children toilet-trained is the single biggest step towards easier travelling. We were very pleased when Kieran made that important step soon after we arrived in Bali on his second visit there.

Cloth Cloth nappies are easy to pack but not as convenient as disposable nappies. For a start they have to be soaked and possibly sterilised with bleach or tea-tree oil, for which you need a bucket. You could take a collapsible camping bucket with you, or take the chance that you can borrow one from your hotel. Don't expect to find sterilising solutions gracing the shelves of the stores in most Asian or African towns and villages. You also have to stay in one place long enough to soak, wash and dry before you move on. Another factor to consider is that the climate may not be conducive to the wearing of plastic pants; in humid conditions fungal infections are common. Woollen or cotton pilchers may be a good alternative.

You will have to carry a minimum of a dozen nappies, and when they get dirty you have to stow them somewhere until you can soak them. The smell of ammonia from urine-soaked nappies can be overwhelming! Despite all that, plenty of travellers with babies do seem to manage with cloth nappies.

Disposable Disposable nappies are very much a commodity of developed countries, but these days you can find them in many developing countries. Of course, they're principally there for visitors rather than local consumption, and this is reflected in the price: you can expect to pay up to US$1 each!

You can try asking the airline of the country you are visiting or the national tourist office but be fairly sceptical of their information. If you need disposable nappies you are much better bringing them with you. Apart from the certainty of actually having them with you they will also be much cheaper back home.

I carried masses of disposable nappies. I calculated how many nappies I use per day, multiplied that number by the number of days I'd be away, added an extra two a day for emergencies and also brought a few cloth nappies with separate waterproof pants as an extra

TRAVEL TIPS...

We would leave home with one large bag full of disposable nappies. As they were used up, the bag could be used to carry purchases.

precaution. We would leave home with one large bag full of disposable nappies. As they were used up, the bag could be used to carry purchases.

Disposable nappies are light so they don't really affect your luggage allowance, they're just bulky. Where possible I let the children disport themselves as nature intended, which conserved the nappies somewhat. It's vital to carry a roll of tape for when the tabs fail as you can't afford to waste them.

Getting rid of disposable nappies is difficult. There is no garbage collection in many developing countries and very often garbage finds its way into the streets or alleyways. I carry plastic bin bags and leave a full, sealed one behind for the hotel to dispose of. I never leave them anywhere else and I just hope the hotel disposes of them properly.

More importantly, be aware that disposable nappies have a long-term environmental impact because they don't break down easily and contribute to the landfill problem, an issue of concern worldwide.

Asia In Asia, countries such as Japan, Singapore and Hong Kong will have nappies readily available. They can be found in major towns or tourist centres in Malaysia, the Philippines, Thailand and Indonesia, with difficulty in large cities in India, and in Colombo in Sri Lanka. In Nepal you'll find them only in Kathmandu and Pokhara, but they are *very expensive*. In Burma, *forget it*. China may begin to produce such luxuries, but for now bring your own.

South America Generally available in big cities in most countries in Central and South America, more widely available in countries like Brazil.

Africa Widely available in South Africa and Zimbabwe and in main centres in touristed countries like Kenya. Very difficult or impossible to buy in the less developed countries.

Port-a-Cots

You can carry your own port-a-cot which airlines will carry free. Some quite sophisticated baby sleeping paraphernalia is available, but with so much extra luggage already you may prefer to simply cope as you go along. In many countries you can get something made if you're going to be staying around long enough or find that life without a carrycot is impossible. We met a family in Bali once who had a beautiful cane bassinet made up.

Bedding

You need two cotton sheets, one warm blanket, a mosquito net (in the tropics), a lambskin or similar 'cuddly'. Of course you don't need to provide all your own bedding wherever you go, but lambskins are a very good idea in that even if the baby sweats a lot they never feel really damp. They are always soft and cuddly and keep a child warm when they are cold and cool when they are hot. You can use lambskins under the sheet as well as on top of it. They are washable but you need a full, hot day to dry them.

For small babies cotton sleeping bags (the type that go on like a nightgown over the head and arms, but fasten down the middle and are sewn along the bottom like a bag) are cooler than sleepsuits, but protect the child from draughts and mosquitoes. Only a soft, light cotton material is necessary. Perhaps (again for small babies) a knitted, woollen bag, or one of the quilted 'pouches' would be a good idea if you plan to go to cooler climates.

Waterproof sheeting is a very good idea for all small children. Even reliably toilet-trained little ones can have an occasional accident when they're very tired or in strange surroundings. Hotels, even cheap ones, generally take this in their stride but you will probably feel better if you carry your own protection.

I usually took the terry/rubber backed type of cot sheet and put it under the sheet. I found it tended to get less hot and sticky than having straight plastic under the sheet. The only problem is remembering to take it with you when you leave the hotel, we 'almost' left ours behind on many occasions. It's worth having a

TRAVEL TIPS...

It's worth having a check list of important things and ticking the list off before you close the bags.

check list of important things and ticking the list off before you close the bags.

I did hear of one family who carried an inflatable mattress for their child to sleep on in order to protect the beds, but I think that may not be too comfortable if you have a child who likes to travel around the bed while asleep. Tashi would have spent most of the night on the floor.

Strollers & Backpacks

A folding, reclining stroller can be a life-saver. We took one on our first long trip with Kieran when we went to Indonesia. At four months he was too young for a backpack carrier but by that time he was too heavy for the front packs. Taking the stroller was easy enough and it was very useful. Obviously, a stroller is no good at all if you plan to go trekking on mountain paths, isolated tracks or beaches. It is strictly useful for day-to-day excursions to the restaurant, shops, hotels and around towns, providing the footpaths are even.

The Indonesians thought the stroller was the most amazing idea: their babies are carried by one or other of the many relatives and neighbours who are always within arm's reach. But when there are only two sets of arms available, one set generally occupied with a bag, and perhaps with another child to contend with, some mechanical means of transport has to be found. The stroller was also great in restaurants. I could strap Kieran in an upright position and eat my meal without having to keep him on my knee – a risky situation – and he was generally content to sit and look around. Because it reclined he could, while he was young, sleep in it so we didn't have to rush back to the hotel when he started hinting it was time for his nap.

The big drawback with strollers is that you need a reasonably smooth surface to push them on. In Western countries this usually presents no problems, but in developing countries rough pavements with missing drain inspection covers and other gaping holes, disintegrating and uneven concrete, rubbish, parked cars, sleeping bodies and steps are just a few of the countless obstacles you are likely to face. Where there is no footpath and you are forced to use the edge of the road, vehicles frequently pass much too close for comfort and your child's face is usually right at the same level as the exhaust pipe! It all combines to make strollers a definite liability in many countries.

Backpacks are good for children who can sit up by themselves. On Kieran's second trip, we went to Nepal and took the backpack rather than the stroller. He was eight months by this time and we did much more walking. For this trip the backpack was more useful with the drawback that he couldn't sleep quite so comfortably in the carrier and it couldn't be used as a chair/restrainer in the restaurant. There are makes of backpacks that can sit up by themselves.

Backpacks may be less useful if you are travelling on you own. If your child starts screaming while in the backpack it is less easy to pacify and you may have to stop and get them out. If there are two of you, one can drop back and talk to the child, give them a drink or distract them. It is also more awkward to use public transport with a child in a backpack. Getting on and off buses or trains and getting seated is usually easier if you carry the baby in your arms and the backpack separately.

There is a combined backpack/stroller on the market which may make life easier. It folds down into a backpack with retractable wheels and, with a bit of fiddling, springs into action as a stroller – quite ingenious.

Feeding Equipment

Bring bottles, teaspoon or baby spoon, plastic dish (wash in boiling water frequently), strainer (tea strainer will do, useful for straining fresh juice), and a plastic juicer. Also, several towelling bibs or a couple of soft plastic ones.

Bring a cup with spout, teaspoon (handy when you are only given a large spoon and fork in a restaurant), plastic bowl (for when you put together a meal yourself, or give them a share of yours). Older children don't require any special equipment unless you are in an area where only chopsticks are used.

Despite the availability of high chairs in many restaurants there are many times when they are not available but you would love to have one. For children who can sit up alone, there are fold-up chairs which suspend from the table. The chairs have nylon or plastic seats and are light and reasonably portable. The problem with these is that they can only be used on certain types of table, and then only if it's strong enough. A stroller can also double as a chair in a restaurant.

PEOPLE

The people will be the most important memories your children take home and you will be surprised at how many they remember. In many countries tourism is definitely a two-way process and often you are the centre of attention. There must be hundreds of photographs of my children adorning the shelves in homes all over the world. Your children are often simply 'borrowed' to complete a photo, because it is best to be photographed in front of the local temple if you are standing next to a foreigner!

Unwanted Attention

The interest in your child can sometimes be negative – many Asians consider children communal property and are used to handing their own children from person to person, to admire and cuddle. They will expect to do the same with yours and while this may be fine up to a point, your child will soon protest when it happens every few minutes. Likewise, a single pinch on the cheek may be OK but 15 or 20 in as many minutes hurts! Gales of laughter if your child shrieks in protest or even bursts into tears don't help either.

TRAVEL TIPS...

...let the children set their own limits and back them up.

Some parents feel their children should learn to cope with such attention because it is part of the culture and it would therefore be rude to refuse to be part of it. Decide how you will handle unwelcome attention. I tend to try and protect the children from it as much as possible because I know I wouldn't like being grabbed by a dozen strangers either! I let the children set their own limits and back them up. I don't try to coax them into being nice to people, although I don't encourage rudeness. If I get questioning looks when my child irritably brushes away an unwanted hand or resolutely turns their back on someone trying to pick them up, I smile sympathetically, shrug my shoulders and pick the child up or put an arm around them. Another way to deal with the problem is to put your children out of reach of curious hands; Tashi loved riding on Tony's shoulders for that reason.

As a teenage traveller, Tashi is re-experiencing the hassles of being stared at and being blonde doesn't help. Teenagers are as self-conscious as toddlers, but more able to defend themselves against unwanted attention.

Local Children

One of the nicest aspects of travelling with young children is that, no matter where you are or what the language is, your children will make friends and communicate beautifully with the local children. In many places older children can be trusted to be responsible for your children if they all go off wandering.

As they get older, children tend to need to have a common language before they can really play together for any length of time. Even a few words can go a long way. We find that our children are frustrated when they can't communicate with other local children, consequently the relationships they strike up now are generally with the children of other travellers. If you do find yourself staying at a hotel where there is another family with children of a similar age you will generally feel you've struck oil – the children will be so delighted to have other children to play with and communicate with that you may not see them from one meal to the next and both sets of parents can take it in turns to mind the children so everyone gets a break. Lunch *à deux* can seem wonderful if every meal for the last month has been a family one.

Despite the communication difficulties children do notice each other and study each others' behaviour. It is interesting to discover what your children are noticing and what they think of it.

The beach is a good place to observe cultural differences and also one of the few places where your children can engage in noisy, boisterous games with the local children without relying on spoken communication. In many places,
in Asia in particular, people come along the beach to sell things and will often sit down for a chat if you have children. Their English may be limited but it can be a good opportunity for a mutual language lesson.

One thing to be aware of on the beach is that although they may splash around happily in the shallows, many local children are not taught to swim. Recreational swimming is not common in many developing countries and even the fishermen who go far out to sea in little sailing boats often cannot swim. Even if your children are good swimmers who don't need close supervision, you have a responsibility to keep an eye on the children they are playing with in case they are led out of their depth and consequently experience difficulties. You may not realise until too late that they are not comfortable in the water.

Kieran liked to travel with a fleet of little cars and vehicles, or various humanoid shapes with which he constructed wonderful games. These would nearly always attract an audience of young local children who were utterly entranced by these 'foreign' objects. At first they would just hang around watching but eventually they couldn't resist picking up the toys and joining in. When Kieran realised they weren't going to steal his toys, and with encouragement from me, they played together for ages, all language difficulties forgotten. Now he's twelve-years-old Kieran's most important travel accessories are his walkman, pencils and drawing pad and a pile of comics and books.

CULTURE

Everywhere you go people seem to like babies; people always want to cuddle a baby and a foreign baby is especially interesting. There are some cultural differences in child rearing and it pays to have a rudimentary knowledge of what they are.

In many Asian countries babies are simply not allowed to cry for long; someone will pick them up the moment they draw breath to yell. This should be borne in mind when your baby decides to let you know that all is not well with their world. You will be expected to do something; it is not good enough to protest that they will soon drop off to sleep and are only crying because they are tired. Babies are to be rocked, cuddled, carried and soothed immediately they show signs of distress, and you will get dirty looks and quite possibly a graphic illustration from an indignant grandmother if your reactions are too slow!

In some cultures older children are not expected to cry: you will be regarded as a weak parent if your children throw tantrums. If you find lose your temper with your children, try not to shout or smack them in public. This may sound very hypocritical, but find some other way to (quietly) defuse the situation. Asians, in particular, don't chastise their children very much, at least in public, and they may be shocked if you do.

Why Asian children are, in general, so well behaved and mature without any overt signs of strong discipline is a mystery to me. As babies they are coddled, taken everywhere, fed on demand, always carried and tended to by one or another of an often large extended family. They sleep with their parents and are rarely excluded from any family happening. They do not have set routines, but sleep when tired and eat when hungry.

From the moment they are walking and talking they are expected to be capable of helping out with family chores and are given increasing responsibility. By five-years-old they may be preparing family meals over open fires, using vicious looking cleavers, looking after babies or helping their parents in the family shop. The boys may be cutting crops with large machetes from age three, without a noticeable increase in limbless people in the population.

Children are taught, quite firmly, what is expected from them and seem to take their place in society with amazing maturity at a very early age. They are treated as if they were small adults and are expected to behave as such. This doesn't stop them from having fun and playing games with gusto, but only when they are with other children; with adults they behave as expected.

Despite having tried to incorporate many of these same child-rearing techniques in raising my own children, I have not managed to achieve this state of maturity with them!

Culture Shock

You may find that your normally outgoing, assertive two-year old becomes very dependent and 'clingy' when you first start travelling. This is normal. When everything familiar has disappeared, what else can they do but hang on to what remains? Don't try to make them 'snap out of it', make friends with strangers or get them to stay with the lovely lady who runs your hotel and is longing for the chance to look after them, you will only make matters worse. Try to be extra comforting, take them with you wherever you go, tell them where you are going and what you hope to see there. Let them know that everything is perfectly normal and fine, and just give them a bit of extra coddling to reassure them. Generally it doesn't take too long for children to regain their sense of security, if handled with understanding.

This 'understanding' may not come easily, especially at the beginning of a trip. If you are also feeling disoriented and a bit uncertain of what you are doing, and if it is your first trip beyond a familiar environment, you may feel a little insecure yourself. Try not to let your children

sense this. Stay close to the hotel, make short walking trips in 'your neighbourhood', eat at the hotel if you feel more comfortable there, and only set off on excursions when you feel ready.

As a parent you are, of course, expected to know everything – you are the source of all wisdom and strength. No matter how vulnerable you are feeling, now is not the time to disillusion your children. Be decisive, even if you are not sure what it is you are deciding. If you need to find out something, ask questions from anyone you meet who is likely to have the information you require. Other travellers you meet in restaurants or on the street are good sources of information regarding places to eat, ways of getting to places, where to change money, etc, and they are usually happy to pass on what they have learned.

At some stage your children, depending on their age, may become upset by the poverty and suffering they see in some countries. Trying to avoid it, or pretending it isn't there, or it isn't so bad, or suggesting that somehow these people are different and don't feel things the same way, is doing your children a disservice and denying them the opportunity to use their travelling experience to its fullest extent. Of course, that doesn't mean that you should launch into a full political and ideological treatise on the Third World; it is generally enough to answer only those questions the children will ask, namely 'why'.

Try to teach your children respect for the people they meet. The best way is by example: be aware of how you speak about the people you meet and how you talk to them. Apart from insisting that the

TRAVEL TIPS...

Stay close to the hotel, make short walking trips in 'your neighbourhood', eat at the hotel if you feel more comfortable there, and only set off on excursions when you feel ready.

standards you normally set are maintained, you must try not to give way to expressions of disdain when you are talking to your partner or other travellers about the local people. This is something we like to think we don't do, but how often does some local frustration cause you to lose your temper or talk about 'these people' in tones of less than affection? Remember that your children use you as their role model, and will rely on you even more now that their world is totally different and their usual guidelines are gone.

The fact that 'grown-up' people don't understand English may cause your children some hilarity; they may feel very superior when someone uses the wrong word or talks 'like babies'. It's a good opportunity to introduce your kids to the language of the country by teaching them a few basic words – 'hello', 'goodbye', 'please', and 'thank you' are good starting points. You can firmly squash such incipient chauvinism by asking them how much of the local language they can speak!

ISRAEL & JORDAN

Ruth Armes & Rod Gibson travelled to Israel & Jordan when Rupert was nearly three years old (pictured on the port bus in Nuweiba).

T HE TRIP DID NOT BEGIN WELL. Rupert got it into his head that he did not like the idea of going on an aeroplane. We dragged him on kicking and screaming, and he continued to scream (and I mean scream) 'Off! Off! I don't like it!' for the next half an hour. Nothing we did or said would pacify him and he just had to sob himself out. We felt awful. So guilty! What were we doing to our poor child? Would he have a plane phobia for the rest of his life? But as things often go with children he soon got interested in his surroundings, perked up no end when the 'bubbles' arrived, and was positively chirpy about the 'tables', 'lunch', and 'telly'. By the time we arrived in Tel Aviv at 7 pm it was as if it had never happened.

That evening we caught a *sherut* (share-taxi) out to Jerusalem's old city. We had selected a hostel out of the guidebook and with map in hand set out to find it. Somehow or other we had misjudged the scale of the map and ended up hopelessly lost wandering around the labyrinth-like alleyways and stairways of the old city. It was not until midnight that we got ourselves safely installed in a room of our own. The Arab owner very kindly produced some pita bread and *hummus* for us.

On our last trip I had found carrying Rupert on my back very wearisome. It was not so much the physical effort, but at the end of the day I simply felt compressed. To add to this it was bothersome constantly getting him in and out of the baby backpack. Rupert, now nearly three-years-old, weighed in at 15 kg. We try to travel very light, one pack between the three of us, a bag of nappies and a backpack to carry Rupert in. So it was after some deliberation that we decided to add a lightweight collapsible stroller to our luggage, even though

23

from previous travelling experience we knew that the pavements in many cities are not suitable. Although terrain did limit its usefulness, it was a lot easier on the occasions when we could use it. On balance it was well worth taking for a toddler.

After a couple of days in Jerusalem we headed north to the Galilee region. The temperature when we got off the air-conditioned bus overwhelmed us. It was a particularly hot day in summer and we had not yet acclimatised. Rupert managed the heat very well. He never ran in the heat and mostly refused to walk as well. We always made sure that he had a beaker of water available and never found we had to worry about his liquid intake. Ensuring that he was smothered in factor 25 sunblock brought about squeals of anguish, but was essential.

We took the official guided tour around the Golan Heights. It was a long day and Rupert had no interest in listening to the guide. We ended up taking it in turns to listen whilst the other found something to amuse Rupert. Usually some stones to throw or a ruin to climb on would suffice. Despite the heat, long coach journeys and boredom Rupert took the experience in his stride and allowed us to get plenty out of the trip. The next day, by way of compensation, we spent on one of the paying beaches by the Sea of Galilee.

We were finding Israel expensive, so rather than eating out we were buying food and cooking on our spirit stove or in the hostel kitchens. Not only cheaper,

Tree of Life, Jericho

it proved easier with Rupert who found it hard to contain his boredom when service was slow in restaurants. We found that eggs and two-minute noodles were available in most supermarkets, which was a quick way of conjuring up a meal we knew Rupert would eat.

Normally we do not take any toys with us, but this time we took two new books and a light weight inflatable football. Throughout our trip Rupert found numerous local children with whom to play football and it was a great success.

From Damascus Gate, Jerusalem, we made a day trip to Massada, timed to allow us to climb to the top to see the dawn. At the bottom Rupert, who was slightly disgruntled at being woken at three in the morning, became ecstatic about the 'big rock'. The journey up with Rupert plus several litres of water on my back was hard, but feasible for anyone who is reasonable fit. The journey back down was rushed because of the need to catch the bus, and the temperature was already rising. I suffered a lot, but on balance the view from the climb and the fortress on the top made the whole experience worthwhile.

On the way back we went for a swim in the Dead Sea. Though a must for every adult, it is no good for small children. The salt water makes every tiny scratch sting like crazy, the slightest splash in your mouth tasted unbelievably foul and I dread to think what getting the stuff in your eyes would feel like.

By now we had heard several stories suggesting that despite having visas issued in the Jordanian Embassy in London and no Israeli stamps in our passports, it was unlikely that we would be able to make the crossing into Jordan. Nevertheless we decided to try to bluff our way across, though we had visions of being stuck in no-man's-land during the heat of day. As it turned out our fears were unfounded and we had no trouble, though the process was time consuming.

From Amman we did a day trip to Jerash to see the Roman ruins. Because of the heat Rupert refused to walk, but when we rested he was quite happy to scrabble about in the dirt. On such occasions we are a little wary of snakes and scorpions, so we usually stamp around a bit first and dissuade him from poking his hands into crevices.

We were sorely tempted to try to hitch down the King's Highway to Petra, but we had heard that there was very little traffic and the prospect of being stuck in the middle of nowhere with Rupert didn't appeal. We shared a service-taxi with an overweight and over generous nun down the Desert Highway to Petra. The next morning we set out to Petra with Rupert in his backpack and five litres of water.

Petra is described as the foremost site in the Middle East. We would rank it amongst the world's best. It was made all the better for being nearly deserted.

We probably did not see more than twenty other tourists in the whole day. We spent eight hours there, six of which Rupert spent in the backpack. He is perfectly content riding in it and never seems to get bored or uncomfortable. Though the archaeology failed to excite him, a pool of mud more than compensated.

We did the climb up to the High Place of Sacrifice. On reaching the altar Rupert became very upset, and would not stop crying until we had descended a little. This was the first time he had cried since getting on the plane, which left us wondering what he had felt up there.

> *Rupert was amused by the bumpy ride in an open truck, and quickly made friends with some Bedouin children when we stopped.*

We made a day trip up to Wadi Rum. Rupert was amused by the bumpy ride in an open truck, and quickly made friends with some Bedouin children when we stopped. Throughout the trip he made friends with the local children. At first he got upset when we left them behind, but he quickly got used to the idea that, 'that is what travelling is about', and soon got into the swing of looking for the next bedroom.

Although the situation has recently changed, whilst we were there it was not possible to cross the border into Israel. It was necessary to catch the ferry to Nuweiba in the Sinai then cross the Egyptian-Israel border. It thus took us a whole day to travel from Aqaba to Eilat. It was perhaps worthwhile though just to experience the hustle and bustle in the port at Aqaba. Fortunately because of Rupert we had 'family status', consequently we were led to the front of all the many queues which it was necessary to stand in to pass through the bureaucratic exit formalities.

Eilat is an expensive beach resort with lots to do if you can afford it. There are quite a few children's activities as well as the good beaches. One day we splashed out and went to the underwater observatory and aquarium. This was a hit with Rupert, especially when we saw a scuba diver swimming around the coral reef.

We returned to Jerusalem for a couple more nights as it was cheaper and cooler. Yassar Arafat was making his first trip to the Gaza Strip and Jericho; as we were entering the Damascus Gate a riot flared up between a group of Jews returning from a demonstration and the local Arab traders. We beat a hasty retreat to the Garden Tomb and spent several pleasurable hours there. The incident served to remind us what living here must be like.

Rod Gibson

SINGAPORE

Peter (pictured with Ruby) & Lorraine Turner travelled to Singapore when Ruby was nearly two years old.

RUBY WAS ALMOST TWO-YEARS-OLD when we decided to cut her teeth on overseas travel. I was researching in Malaysian Borneo for *Malaysia, Singapore & Brunei – travel survival kit*, but even though parts of Borneo are very civilised these days, Lorraine and I decided that it was better to try Ruby out in Singapore first. All the necessities for travel with children were on hand: efficient transportation, comfortable hotels, potable water, good food, disposable nappies and Valium (it may come in handy for parents). Singapore was for the most part as safe and easy as travel at home.

Our big predeparture quandary was whether to take the stroller or not. After much deliberation, we decided that Singapore's 'five-foot ways' weren't compatible with strollers. 'Five-foot ways' are the roughly five-feet-wide verandas at the front of Chinese shops, and each shop is usually on a different level, so walking is a constant up or down and pushing a stroller is nigh on impossible on these traditional walkways. Singapore's modern streets now have plenty of level pavements, but even Singapore's increasingly wealthy and consumer-minded middle class haven't found it necessary to acquire Emmalungas, the Rolls-Royce of prams, with good reason we figured.

I flew into Singapore from Borneo and easily amused myself in Changi airport for a few hours while I waited for Lorraine's and Ruby's flight to arrive.

I wondered how Ruby would take to Singapore, and worried that she might be allergic to travel. What if she broke out in a rash from foreign bedding, convulsed whenever she ventured away from air-conditioning or vomited at the very thought of bus travel? On the other hand, Ruby was at an ideal age to travel. She was old enough to walk and communicate her basic needs, pre-tantrum but post-breastfeeding, cognisant but still mystified by the magic of a world that adults take for granted. Above all, at her age she could still fly for only 10% of a full adult airfare.

My biggest worry was that she wouldn't recognise me. After weeks in Borneo, I might be just another 'uncle', one of those adults who appear in from time to time and pretend to be interested in you but can't even remember your name.

> **'...then she saw the hotel bed, jumped up and down and ordered me to "Play, Dad!" She remembered me. '**

On arrival Ruby allowed herself to be kissed, staring somewhere just over my shoulder. Lorraine had to go and deal with some ticketing hassles and left Ruby sitting on my lap. She sat placidly admiring the Changi Airport architecture while I talked to her. We caught a taxi to the hotel and Ruby was still unimpressed by my presence, but then she saw the hotel bed, jumped up and down and ordered me to 'Play, Dad!' She remembered me.

Singapore has plenty to keep kids amused. The government backed and directed tourism industry is very aware that Singapore is a family destination and 'Tourism Inc' is keen to promote and develop attractions for the family. The tourist office produces a good booklet *Family Fun Island*, outlining attractions. Family attractions are mostly theme parks and the grandaddy of all Singapore's theme parks is Sentosa Island.

Sentosa has fun rides, museums, water sports, aquariums, a monorail, cable car, etc for the family to enjoy. Ruby was just a bit too young to appreciate most of the attractions but the nature trail was certainly exciting. All over Asia pesky little monkeys hang out at temples and parks waiting for scraps of food from visitors, and if they don't get them watch out! The cute little monkey that Ruby was admiring suddenly became an aggressive little bastard, lunged at her and grabbed the strawberry milk she was holding. He was up a tree in a flash, guzzling from the carton and dribbling pink liquid down his chest. Despite her fear at the time, Ruby still retells the story with delight and in years to come it will probably be her only memory of that trip to Singapore.

In Singapore, like in most Asian countries, restaurants tend to be noisy, communal affairs and exuberant children are not seen as destroyers of conversation and appetite. This is in contrast to Australian restaurants where children are not only regarded as aberrant, anti-social creatures, somewhere beneath

travel stories

smokers in contempt, but there has even been suggestions that children should be banned from restaurants.

By far the best place to take children is to the food centres. Not only can you get a complete range of all Singapore's cuisine at cheap prices but children can roam freely, make plenty of noise and not be noticed in the clamour. The Newton Circus food centre, not far from Orchard Rd, is a good place to take children. It is a slightly more upmarket, tourist-oriented food centre. It is a pleasant, open-air centre in the evenings with plenty of room for kids to run around.

Shopping is one of Singapore's main attractions and kids are also well catered for. The Forum Galleria on Orchard Rd has many shops dedicated to children, selling designer children's clothing and toys. The main shop here is the large Toys 'R Us store, where we managed to prise Ruby away from a $500 toy car and escaped with only a $10 teddy to add to Ruby's already huge collection of teddy bears.

> **❝ *"What a waste," he said smiling, as if the disappointment of having a girl was a self-evident truth.* ❞**

Though Singapore has a rather cold image as a soulless, money-making society, the family is sacred and, indeed, family values are enshrined in law (the paternalistic government's latest proposals will allow parents to sue errant children who refuse to support them). Children are doted on, and Ruby received plenty of attention. Above all, her red hair was a show stopper. Wandering around the backstreets of Chinatown, every Chinese grandmother went out of their way to stroke Ruby's hair or pinch her cheeks. The Malays and Indians are no less fond of children. In one shop in Little India, Ruby had everyone in the shop admiring her.

'So cute. Is this your first?' said the shop owner.

'Yes.'

'And is it a boy or a girl?'

'A girl.'

'What a waste,' he said smiling, as if the disappointment of having a girl was a self-evident truth.

Peter Turner

NEPAL

*Hugh Finlay &
Linda Henderson
travelled for a
month in Nepal
when Ella was six
& Vera 2½.*

A S PART OF MY 'REGULAR' ROUND OF UPDATING, I was involved with the new edition of *India – travel survival kit*, and so was returning there for the update. In the past Linda – both alone and with our first daughter, Ella – had joined me for parts of my trips. It was less than an ideal arrangement as I had to travel fast, had much to do and was not able to spend much time relaxing with them. As a result we decided this time to have a 'proper' holiday (ie, one where I wasn't working at the same time) in Nepal.

Both myself and Linda had travelled and trekked extensively in Nepal – without kids – and thought it would be a good place to return to with our two children – Ella aged six and Vera 2½-years-old. It turned out to be an excellent choice, although there were moments when we doubted our sanity in carting two kids half-way across the world, exposing them to all manner of bugs and diseases, not to mention the pollution of Kathmandu, just so we could see some mountains with snow on them. At times Ella was inclined to agree: 'What's so special about them, Dad?', was her response at one stage, after having the snow-capped mountains pointed out to her by excited parents for the fifth time in as many minutes on the spectacular plane ride between Kathmandu and Pokhara.

We were off to a good start; on the taxi ride into Kathmandu from the airport both the kids were goggle-eyed at the number of 'farm' animals on the streets: 'Hey Dad, there's a cow on the road!', but the amazement grew: 'Ha, it's eating a cardboard box!'. Sheep, goats and chickens were all sighted regularly. That's one thing about Asian cities which makes them so interesting to travel in: they may be hectic but there's never a dull moment, and even a walk along a street can be a revelation for curious youngsters.

Finding a suitable hotel in Kathmandu was not a problem, although we were not paying rock-bottom prices. When travelling without kids we used to stay in some pretty awful dives, usually for one simple reason: price. These days price seems less important than family-friendly places with features that can keep kids happier for longer and therefore increase the chances of us actually surviving without going bananas – the place we settled in charged US$20 for a spacious, carpeted triple room with attached bathroom complete with bathtub and hot water. The icing on the cake was the spacious (and child-safe) 5th-floor roof garden, where we could eat and relax and the kids could let off steam without annoying anyone – well not too much anyway.

Kathmandu's narrow streets and quite heavy traffic made walking around with the kids something of a chore, and one which we chose to avoid whenever possible by taking cycle-rickshaws. The only problem here was that the cycle-rickshaw wallahs had become soft – and greedy – from too many easy tourist fares! Anything more than a km or so was considered too much, and their first quoted fares were laughable. They were quite happy for us to follow the local custom and crowd four of us into the two-seater rickshaw though.

We were warmly received everywhere. On one walk around Kathmandu we stopped at a tiny cafe for a snack of *momos* – excellent steamed pastry envelopes stuffed with meat. The cafe was run by a Tibetan family and the *momos* were made right at the front. Our kids were soon involved with rolling out the small pastry circles and having a great time. It was only with the bribe of an ice cream that we were able to extract them without a major scene. The cafe became a regular haunt of ours as we knew the girls would be kept amused.

The only problem with encounters with local people perhaps is that they can be a bit over the top at times. By the end of the trip both our kids were fed up with being poked, prodded and generally fussed over, but the thing that really pissed Ella off was the way she was invariably greeted: 'Hello, baby'. At nearly six years old she felt entitled to something a little more appropriate! Vera liked to retreat to the safety of my shoulders or the backpack. This kept her up out of the way of prodding fingers (and stray dogs), and it also made her much bolder; from the safety of her perch she would pull horrible faces and generally show off to all and sundry.

One of the main goals of our trip was to do a week-long trek in the mountains. Many people we spoke to thought it was perhaps a bit of an ambitious thing to undertake with two small children, but this just made us more determined to give it a go – we could always turn back if it didn't work out. Our base point was to be Pokhara, seven bumpy and dusty but cheap hours by bus, or one easy, spectacular and not too expensive hour by plane (we opted for the latter) from Kathmandu.

> **'...they would disappear into the candle-lit, smoky interiors of the kitchen, and usually emerge beaming some time later, clutching a boiled potato or some other morsel...'**

We approached many of the trekking agencies, and finally settled on one which we felt had its act together sufficiently to arrange for porters and transport to the trail head. Our plan was that we would have three porters – two to carry rucksacks, and a third to carry Vera most of the time, and Ella when she got tired of walking. As it turned out, Ella walked virtually the whole way, which was a damn good effort, and Vera was carried in a large, conical, cane basket on one of our porter's back. Once again she felt safe being up off the ground, and made her customary ugly faces at trekkers and locals we passed along the trail. Her mode of travel certainly made her a curiosity to locals and foreigners alike. To wedge her in safely we sat her first in her backpack, placed this in the basket, and then filled the gaps with sleeping bags and items of warm clothing we shed as the day wore on. The porters were great with the kids, and although we felt a bit like a travelling show at times, it was worth hiring enough porters to free us of any major load.

Overall the trek went very well, but we realised early on that we had overestimated how far we would be able to walk in one day. Once we slowed

travel stories

down and basically let Ella set the pace, things were fine. The walking itself was not too strenuous, largely because of our slow pace, but we did get up to 3500 metres, and even at this altitude the children's breathing was affected.

Staying in the tea houses along the way was a highlight for the kids. On arrival they would disappear into the candle-lit, smoky interiors of the kitchen, and usually emerge beaming some time later, clutching a boiled potato or some other morsel kindly given by the hard-working women of the house.

The major problem we faced on the trek was a bout of giardia which Vera contracted, and this led to our second biggest problem: what to do with all the soiled disposable nappies. They're a bugger of a thing to get rid of at the best of times; in small villages in the mountains they are a disaster.

Empty plastic mineral water bottles are another problem in the mountains, and it's recommended that you buy iodine tablets and purify your water that way. Some powdered flavouring helps to disguise the awful taste, but our two steadfastly refused anything other than plain bottled water.

Perhaps the most difficult aspect of the trip was one we least expected: eating out. Nepal's restaurants are famous for their wonderful food, but it does often take an awfully long time to arrive. Keeping two weary kids amused for half an hour or more while we waited was a chore, especially with the accompaniment of 'Where's my *dinner*!'. Although there was plenty of variety, when the food did finally arrive the kids would only pick at it. In the end we'd go into a restaurant, immediately order two bowls of banana porridge, and then take our time to order our own food. The locals seemed to think that porridge for dinner was some Western aberration, but at least it was quick and got eaten.

Would we do it again? No hesitation.

Hugh Finlay

ARGENTINA

María Massolo and Wayne Bernhardson took their daughter Clío (pictured at Merlo when 2½) to Argentina to research the LP guide to the region.

A RGENTINA IS EXTREMELY CHILD-FRIENDLY in terms of people's attitudes, safety and health, and family-oriented activities, although there are regional differences. When Wayne and I did the research for *Argentina, Uruguay & Paraguay – travel survival kit*, our daughter Clío was 2½-years-old and we took her with us on the road part of the time; she also returned there for an entire year at the age of four.

We thought that since Clío was a good walker, we did not need a stroller. In retrospect that was a serious mistake. If we had had our folding stroller she would have been able to rest or take naps in it instead of in our arms or on our shoulders. Furthermore, in museums it would have been a good way of keeping track of her. Argentina is not a place where children risk kidnapping, but there is always the chance of getting lost in crowds.

Even if a child gets lost, someone will try to help. One afternoon Clío left our apartment in downtown Buenos Aires, went downstairs, and out the door into the street. The minute she stepped out, the heavy iron and glass door closed behind her. By the time I realised she was gone and rushed downstairs, I could see her crying outside as a formally dressed young man, gently calming her down, asked her if she remembered the apartment number to ring the bell. Clío was relieved to see me.

People are also very helpful on public transport; often someone will give up a seat for a parent and child, but if that does not occur, an older person may offer to put the child on her or his lap. Sometimes this happens in such an spontaneous way that you find someone pulling a child out of your arms. Remember, this is a country where people frequently touch each other (to get someone's attention you may touch him or her on the arm and say '*Disculpe...*'), so your children will be patted on the head, or caressed quite a bit.

In terms of food and health, there are no major concerns in most parts of Buenos Aires, but we usually drank bottled water. In general this had to do more with the horrible taste of chemicals and chlorine of the tap water than with health risks. Basic restaurants provide a wide selection of food suitable for children (vegetables, pasta, meat, chicken, fish); however, we rarely ordered a separate dish for Clío – Argentine portions are abundant, so we always shared with her. Waiters have no problem bringing an extra dish and cutlery, although in some places they may charge extra for providing them. The real treat for all of us, particularly in the warm months, was Argentina's superb ice cream, with a tremendous variety of both fruit (juice based) and creamy flavours. Clío also loves the local croissants for breakfast; they are small and come in sweet and unsweetened varieties.

> *At all times we had a bed ready for Clío , with her "special" blanket, so when she got tired of playing games or singing with us, she rested or slept comfortably.*

Our main concern was bathrooms. Public toilets in general are often poorly kept, so we avoided them as much as possible. On the occasions that Clío could not wait, I held her so she would not touch the toilet. Always carry toilet paper with you, since it is non-existent in public lavatories. Moreover, while a woman may take a young boy into the ladies' room, it would be socially unacceptable to take a girl to a men's room.

Unless you are travelling by plane, remember that distances are long and trips seem never ending. We were lucky enough to have a truck with a camper shell open to the cab. At all times we had a bed ready for Clío , with her 'special' blanket, so when she got tired of playing games or singing with us, she rested or slept comfortably. Similarly, we would prepare a bed for her in buses and trains (only occasionally running nowadays).

In Argentina breastfeeding in public is very much related to ethnicity; in the more indigenous areas women breastfeed their babies in the markets, but I don't recall ever seeing a mother breastfeeding in public in Buenos Aires. However, there is always the possibility of going to a cafe, and covering yourself with a baby blanket. The drawback in this case, of course, would be the inevitable cigarette smoke.

travel stories

Clío loves Buenos Aires, a city whose size and fast pace fascinate her; the Obelisco, a downtown landmark, gives her a reassuring sense of familiarity. We used to make her find it from a bus or taxi, or in our walks, and make her guess if someone was looking from the tiny window at the top. Her joy was great early one morning when she saw a city maintenance worker enter the tower through a door at its base.

Buenos Aires offers a good selection of children's cultural activities – theatre, movies, music – that are listed in a special newspaper column. More of these activities take place during winter school recess (early to mid July) but they are also very crowded. We tried to balance indoor activities and museum visits, which were tiring for all of us, by spending time at open spaces like the Plaza Francia near Recoleta, where she could use the playground, or the Plaza de Mayo, where she could chase pigeons.

If in Buenos Aires children are liked, in the interior they are treated like royalty. One of the hardest rules for Clío was to be polite and accept candy from passersby with a *gracias* but not to eat it. Elderly people, men in particular, would often carry candy and give it to passing children; their intentions are good, but we always made her put it in the nearest garbage can. Visiting a family is even more problematic; in most cases children will be offered candy, sodas, or sweets: 'health food' is an alien concept. When we felt she had had too much, we solved the problem by telling white lies like: 'she has a problem with sugar so the doctor recommends keeping it to a minimum'.

In parts of northern Argentina cholera is a problem, and although government rhetoric often tried to minimise it, we played safe by not eating uncooked vegetables or unpeeled fruits, and using mineral water even to brush our teeth. Regional foods, like *empanadas*, tend to be spicier than in the central or southern parts of the country, so there Clío ate much more pasta and grilled meats. Hotel employees never denied us boiling water, and often in budget hotels we were able to use their kitchen and make pasta or soups.

Unlike Buenos Aires, where life moves really fast, the provincial cities enjoy a calmer, healthier pace, where the afternoon siesta finds usually lively town centres virtually abandoned. Even in later trips, at five-years-old, Clío found this rhythm more suited to her needs.

In general Argentina is a great country to travel with children. Its child-friendly culture makes a family welcome in most places, and its modern amenities facilitate travelling. Some camping grounds, for instance, have secure playgrounds where children make instant friendships, transcending language or cultural barriers.

María Massolo

GETTING THERE & AROUND

AIR

There's more than a hint of truth in the saying, there are just two classes of travel – 1st class and with children. Flying with children can be an endurance test.

I always loved flying: give me a window seat, a few magazines or books, headset, movie, food, a few glasses of wine – bliss. To me the excitement of going places is connected with airports and planes. Children changed all that.

Babies

With babies, flying is generally more difficult than with older children, simply because you have to work so hard to keep them happy – nursing them, playing with them, singing to them. And if you don't keep them happy they cry, then see how friendly your neighbours are! Add to this the strain of changing nappies in the cramped toilets and the difficulties of eating your meal with a baby on your knee and you may decide to stay home!

Toddlers

Toddlers are hard-going as travel companions; a long flight can be pure torture for an 18-month to three-year-old, not to mention the parents. Whilst a baby may be kept happy by your proximity and undivided attention, herculean efforts are required to amuse and distract toddlers; books, toys and snacks can only go so far, usually not more than a few hours. Hopefully all their misspent energy will result in a long sleep, but don't count on it!

Older Children

From three or four years on it does get easier. The children can amuse themselves with drawing and simple games. They can play with a few well-chosen toys, listen through headphones to the children's' channel, and even the movie will put in a little time. They can feed themselves, with supervision, from their tray and the novelty of being offered drinks will usually keep them in good humour. It is also easier to persuade them to lie down and have a sleep.

Teenagers

Now, with children aged 12 and 14-years-old flying has regained some of its previous enjoyment.

Fares & Baggage Allowance

Children under two years old pay 10% of the full adult fare on international flights, provided they are accompanied by a fare-paying adult. Only one 10% fare is allowed per adult, any other children have to pay the children's fare. Children on 10% fares do not get a seat (they're expected to sit on your lap if necessary) or any baggage allowance. Nor do they get a meal; you're supposed to bring food for them or let them pick off your tray.

Children's fares in relation to adult's fares vary to some extent. In general it seems that children are classified as from two to 12 years of age for international flights, and three to 12 years of age for domestic flights. Children usually pay 50% of the scheduled adult fare or 67% of discount fares, which account for a high proportion of fares these days. The age of the child at the time of departure is the determining factor; if your child passes the critical age while you're away that's no problem. Once your child has turned 12 all the discounts end; they're full fare or adult from then on.

Airlines usually make an effort to ensure that if the flight is less than full, passengers with small children are given the benefit of spare seats. Similarly, necessary items for the baby during the flight can be brought on as cabin luggage. 'Necessary items' can be loosely interpreted, although it generally means food, nappies and clothes. Most (but not all) airlines will allow a pusher/stroller to be carried onto the plane. And it's very rare that there isn't a spare meal or two left over at meal times.

Although you cannot, officially at least, bring a baby's carrycot on board, the airlines will usually carry it free. They ask that it be collapsible if possible, but as long as it doesn't exceed 76 by 40

by 30 cm that's OK. They don't specify what carrycots can weigh but as long as it's not over about 10 kg you should have no problems.

Children (but not infants on a 10% fare) do get the full baggage allowance and if you're travelling somewhere tropical, where your clothes and baggage requirements are lightweight, you may find yourself with lots of spare baggage allowance. This can be very useful if you wish to bring back a large piece of local exotica. On a couple of occasions we've managed to come back from Bali with quite large stone carvings as part of our luggage. Coming back from Mexico, where the baggage allowance is by the piece rather than by weight, four of us times two pieces each would have given us enough room to start a small Mexican crafts shop!

Sometimes in Asia the regulations have to be played around with, for reasons other than economics. Once in Nepal we were trying to get on a flight from Pokhara back to Kathmandu. We were told there were not enough seats – unless Tashi was under two? 'Yes', we said, with very straight faces, even though Tashi was only days away from being three, several sizes larger than the average Nepalese two-year-old and very obviously not a toddler.

Service

Airlines and airports offer quite a range of services and in general are very sympathetic to travelling parents', and their children's, needs. Some airlines really are better than others at catering for children, some give the distinct impression that the flight attendants' training is much more heavily inclined towards pouring the wine properly rather than coping with toddlers.

It's quite easy to see the airlines that do think about children and their parents and often a little thought is much more appreciated than all the free colouring books.

At the end of the day, however, no amount of cheerful, competent, well thought out service can match lots of empty seats around you. The least crowded flights are often the very best ones as far as flying with children is concerned. With a couple of seats to stretch over, small children can sleep just as comfortably as they do at home. A good flight route can make a real differ-

---

HELPFUL AIRLINE SERVICE

In a perfect world airlines would provide the following service:

Pre-Board Small Children & Parents You start the trip on the wrong foot if you have to queue for ages getting to your seat, fighting your way down a crowded aisle with your carry-ons, your children's carry-ons and (if it's an odd-hours departure) quite possibly sleepy or bad tempered children as well.

Supply Children's Meals on Request Most airline food is unsuitable for children – it just doesn't accord with their tastes. Some American airlines will provide chicken & chips or sausages & chips which are much more appetising for most children.

Serve Children's Meals First It takes very little effort for the flight attendants to bring all the small children their meals before they start the general meal service. That way your child can have got their meal out of the way before yours even arrives, and you're not stuck with trying to cope with two precariously balanced meals at once.

Treat Children as Human Beings On vacation-time flights I always appreciate the captain who prefaces announcements with 'ladies and gentlemen, boys and girls'. Older children love flight deck visits which some airlines manage to put on during the flight and a good children's channel on the entertainment system can be a real life saver on long flights. Some airlines even have activities books which tie in with the children's channel.

ence as well: children dislike being woken up in the middle of the night in order to stand around some God-forsaken airport terminal even more than adults do.

Arrive at the airport early and try to be among the first to check in. This is important if you are going to have any choice at all in the seat allocation, although airlines often will try to give families more choice than other passengers.

All airlines carry bassinets on their long-distance flights, but they are only useful for very young babies. Pillows and blankets are also available.

Special diets, such as non-salted, low cholesterol, vegetarian, kosher, diabetic, etc, should be booked at least 48 hours in advance. If you require snacks rather than full meals for your child or yourself, you can book this with the airline. You can also order baby food, or bring it yourself and they will heat it up.

The only problem with leaving everything to the airlines is that you may not always be able to get what you want when you need it. For instance, your plane is leaving just at the time your children are usually going to bed, and you may have to leave home mid-afternoon. The ideal time to feed your children is probably when you are sitting in the departure lounge. If you have some sandwiches, fruit or a yoghurt you can have a picnic dinner there and then, or you could buy them a meal at the airport. Otherwise, by the time you're up and flying, the pre-dinner drinks have been served and meal time finally rolls round it's going to be far beyond any possibility of a civilised meal!

Similarly, your children may be hungry before dinner arrives and the cabin crew may be able to organise special meals. If you have something in your bag for them to nibble on you can stop the demands before they become too vocal. I usually hang on to the crackers and cheese that come with airline dinners just in case they're needed at some other time.

Airports

Most airports have a parents' room where you can change and feed your baby; some are excellent, others are inconvenient and dismal. There has been a swing towards making these facilities available to 'parents' rather than 'mothers', so these days fathers too can change and tend to their babies.

More airports are starting to cater for older children as well – Singapore's Changi Airport, rated by many as the best in the world, actually has a wonderful play area for kids in the transit/departure area. There is even a series of science exhibits which children can manipulate and have fun with. Amsterdam's airport is equally well-equipped for children.

Equipment for the Flight

There is a fine balance between bringing everything you can possibly think of that your child might need, and what you really do need.

Babies Bring something for babies to sleep on: a rug, lambskin or a 'cuddly'. See the Sleeping section in this chapter for information on 'beds'. Bring enough cloth or disposable nappies to last the journey; airlines do carry disposable nappies but it is best to consider those as an emergency supply only. For cleaning bring 'wet wipes', a damp cloth in a plastic bag, lotion and cotton wool or whatever else you like to use. A few bibs are a very good idea.

Plastic bin liners are good for storing any dirty nappies, dirty clothes, wipes, etc, until you can dispose of them. Usually the crew will take them away, but you can't expect them to be there right when you need them, and it is less offensive to be handed a plastic bag containing a nasty object rather than the nasty object itself.

A waterproof change mat is useful. Although there is usually one toilet in each section with a fold-down change table, I really have never found them to be very useful. How do you hold a wriggling child down on a flat, hard surface in a cramped aeroplane toilet and change a nappy at the same time? I find it easier to lay the mat on my seat and change the baby there, unless it is really too disgusting and likely to make me very unpopular with other passengers.

At least one change of clothing is necessary. Depending on the age of your baby, a few toys may also help. For children under six months the people around them may provide enough interest. For children over six months toys that they can fiddle with seem to keep them occupied for a little while. Don't bring toys with lots of bits; you don't want to spend the flight picking up pieces from the floor. Don't bring too many toys either – a handful of tried and true favourites are all that is necessary.

You may like to consider taking a

WHAT TO BRING
Babies & Toddlers

lambskin, rug, cuddly
disposable nappies
change(s) of clothing/underpants
wet wipes, mopping up cloth
food, drinks
spoons, dish
bibs
bottle(s)
plastic bags
waterproof change mat

---

plastic reclining infant seat – the type with the adjustable stand and handles at each side – a useful item for carrying small babies onto planes, equally useful for feeding them in and for getting them out of your arms for a while. But it may also be a nuisance to carry around on your travels.

Toddlers For children from 12 months up, you can start shedding some of the equipment. For long flights I would still bring something for sleeping on or with, and at least one change of clothes. For those out of nappies take at least a couple of pairs of pants; accidents happen even to 'trained' children when they are excited, or worse, have to wait in line too long for a vacant toilet. Wet wipes are still very useful, as is a general 'mopping up' cloth.

Toys and books are useful, but bear

in mind the limitations. Pipe cleaners make unusual toys; they can be twisted into shapes and can make little people. Favourite dolls and teddies of course must be included, and coloured pencils and notepads to draw on. The cabin crew usually hand out games, books, pencils, etc, when your children get on the plane. Thai International got top marks on one particular flight for a plastic bib which went on to cover many miles with Tashi and was really useful (Kieran got one on his 'maiden flight' also). They also gave out 'stickle bricks' to older children which is an excellent toy and passed many happy hours both on the plane and off. Many of the give-aways are pitched at an older age group but children are almost always pleased at getting things for free, and will always find something that can be used.

One very useful hint was passed on by my mother-in-law. Most children have a 'familiar' that must travel with them – a teddy, or a doll, or some such friend. To avoid having to carry this, and the baby, and the bags, tie elastic around its neck, so that there is a loop. This loop goes around your child's wrist. It means that even if you do have to carry teddy, the elastic loop can go around your wrist, or over the stroller handle, and still leave your hands free. This tactic prevents the nightmarish possibility that you may inadvertently leave it behind somewhere.

Other methods for coping with small children at airports include attaching a small but loud whistle to your children's' jacket. If they get lost or even momentarily separated from you, they can give a good piercing blast. It gives them a sense of security, although you will probably have to dissuade them from using it at inappropriate moments and hope they remember to use it at the appropriate one! Some people find toddlers' reins useful at the airport or other crowded places. I did try reins once or twice but it's a battle to get children to wear them and I didn't persevere.

Older Children As children get older the problems dwindle, although on long flights they get bored, just as adults do. Bring adequate supplies of books, toys and games. A walkman with story and music tapes is a great idea because it keeps the children happy and quiet, but thankfully can't be heard by the parents. Our children have made lots of international flights now and although they dislike being cooped up just as much as the next child they've never been any real problem.

Comfort Finally, planes are very dry, and this can make everyone feel uncomfortable. I like to take a spray can of Evian Mineral Water to spray on their faces; it feels nice and fresh and the children usually think it is a lot of fun, and if you follow it with a moisturising cream, it does take the tight, dry feeling away. A chap stick is also useful for dry lips.

Toothbrushes and toothpaste are good for when you want to freshen up. They are also a good idea for the children, who invariably end up drinking more soft drinks and sweetened juice than you would normally allow.

If you find the dry air causes sore noses or sinus discomfort, try putting a

WHAT TO BRING
Older Children

trainer cup (cup with spout)
coloured pencils & notepads
games
books
mineral water spray
moisturising cream
chap stick
toothbrushes & toothpaste
change of clothes or top
plastic bags
wet wipes/cloth

scarf or handkerchief around their faces, like a bandit. Something made of light material, lightly placed across their noses may cause some localised humidity and ease the discomfort. I try to put the blanket lightly over their faces when they are asleep.

Food & Drink

If your baby takes a bottle, then bring the bottle and at least most of the food needed. Although airlines will provide baby food upon request, it is best to be self-sufficient; if there are more babies than expected on the flight supplies of nappies and food can be quickly depleted. Also you may get held up somewhere unexpectedly and your supplies may have to go further than planned, so take what you calculate you need and perhaps a bit more. For quick, easy feeding on planes and in airports, bring jars of baby food, rather than cans. Two spoons (one for you to feed them with, one for them to feed themselves) and a plastic dish are also a good idea, although you can feed them straight from the jar if you discard any uneaten portion.

In many developing countries domestic flights don't operate to the same standards as international services. It may be a good idea not to ask the crew to wash your bottles or make up formula. Try to bring enough clean bottles to last the journey. Although the water is generally purified, it is best to be on the safe side. It's not uncommon to see signs on aircraft water supplies warning you that you should not drink the water other than from the water fountains.

If your baby is breastfed, you should still bring some juice and a bottle. Babies need to drink quite a lot during the flight because the atmosphere is so dehydrating, and nursing mothers may feel they seem to be continuously feeding. Giving the baby frequent drinks of juice and water are a good idea to give the mother a break. The little bottles of juice for babies which are designed to take a standard feeding teat are a good idea. They are sealed until you need them, you just take off the top and replace it with a teat and usually there is just the right amount there. You don't have to worry about leakages, or juice spoiling.

Everyone gets dehydrated on planes, so nursing mothers have to be especially careful to increase their fluid intake (not alcohol or caffeine though). Use the water fountains frequently or request glasses of mineral water.

Airline meals are generally very

much inclined towards adult tastes and often children will do no more than pick at them. Check when you book your ticket if they will supply a snack or children's meal. Juice is freely available, as are soft drinks, but if you prefer not to give your children juice with sugar or preservatives you will have to bring it with you. The small bottles of baby juice are very conveniently sized, even for older children, and are sugarless and without preservatives.

One very important item for this age group is a trainer cup (one with a spout). These were so useful I always packed two, just in case one got lost along the way. Drinking juice or anything out of plastic cups is quite a difficult feat for small children; it invariably ends up on you, them, your seat or, if you're lucky, the floor. If you just make a blanket rule that while on the plane all drinks must be drunk from the spout cup, your trip will be much drier.

If you do decide to bring snacks remember they will be spending quite a while in your bag; anything with a tendency to mush, crumble or sog is not a good idea. I'm afraid I leave my food principles behind when I fly with the children. I bring a large bag of sweets with which I bribe, cajole and cheer up when necessary.

Sleeping

All airlines carry a few bassinets on their long-distance flights; but they are only useful for very young babies. The bassinet either clips on to the bulkhead (the front wall of the cabin) or hangs above your head on certain designated seats in the window aisle.

Their dimensions are between 58 and 70 cm long and about 30 cm wide, and about 20 cm deep and are supposed to be for babies up to 10 kg: if your baby is an average size or bigger it can be very cramped to lie in. They do, however, give you an area for a baby to sit and play in. If you require a bassinet you must reserve it when you book your ticket.

Both my children slept on lambskins as babies, so I always brought them on the plane with me. They are bulky, but can be easily folded down into normal cabin luggage and it can be very useful on long flights to have something familiar and comforting for children to sleep on. If your children have a favourite rug or blanket, bring it with you if possible.

For older children it doesn't seem to matter; they will settle down and sleep when they are ready, and the flight attendant will bring blankets and pillows to make them comfortable. You can only hope for an extra seat so the children can stretch out to make life really easy!

Pillows and blankets are available on board from the overhead lockers. Although they are usually only handed out on night flights you can always ask a flight attendant for extra pillows and blankets.

Seating

Where you sit can be quite important. Parents with small children are generally placed in the first row of seats facing the bulkhead on the theory that there is more leg room. Well, there may be, but on many aircraft the bulkhead seat row has fixed armrests which the tables fold down into, which means that if you are lucky enough to score a vacant seat beside you, your child can't lie out flat because the armrest won't budge. Even if there is no vacant seat, if the armrest won't lift you can't spread your child across their seat and your knee.

Another reason I usually avoid the bulkhead is because when the movie is on you are right beneath it and it is harder to persuade a child to sleep when the flickering images are right above. Also if you stand up, which you seem to have to do a lot with children, you are in everyone's way. It is also less easy to turn your light on for all those emergencies for which you need illumination, as this affects the picture for everyone behind. Finally, any other parents with babies will be right there with you. Who needs someone else's problems? If your children don't usually cry, sitting beside children who do cry might just set them off!

If it is to be a long flight I try to ask for seats in the middle section, between the two aisles, on the theory that there are more seats in that section than between the aisle and the window, so you have more chance of being able to stretch out if there are vacant seats. The cabin crew are generally very helpful and understanding and will try to find you extra seats if at all possible. Also if you and your family have three seats in a row of four and an individual stranger sits down in the remaining seat, one look at your contingent is usually enough to send them looking for alternative seating, so you may still wind up with an extra seat. If you have two adults and two or more children you can always go on a scouting trip through the plane; you may find that by splitting up you can get very comfortably organised for sleeping.

Sedation

Sedating children for flights is a tricky question. I don't like to use any medication unless absolutely necessary, but when the children were smaller I found that no matter how tired they were they could keep themselves awake through sheer excitement, and once they got beyond a certain point they were miserable, cranky and exhausted, but still not asleep. Some children simply sleep when they are tired, but not all. On the occasions that I did use sedatives I found them very helpful; the children arrived in much better shape to cope with the first few days in a new place, and we didn't have a fraught flight.

Another consideration is that if you have spent too many hours awake with your children you will also be pretty exhausted and unable to deal with them with the patience necessary to help them to settle in. Your doctor can probably advise you on what to give them. I used Phenergan (promethazine), an antihistamine which is useful for travelling as it can help combat travel sickness. A 10 mg tablet worked fine for Kieran at 18 months, but it took 25 mg for four-year-old Tashi. The tablets are small enough for very young children and can be given in a spoonful of jelly or whatever. The alternative of 25 ml of Phenergan liquid is much more difficult to get down them.

You must give them the sedative before they reach the totally miserable stage as it may be too late to have much effect later.

Now that the children are older I don't find it necessary to use anything to help them sleep and even if they don't sleep on shorter flights neither makes a fuss or causes problems for anyone else.

TRAVEL TIPS...

Get to the airport in time to organise everything and everyone calmly.

Preparation for the Flight

It is a good idea to plan for a calm, relaxed day for the 24 hours before your flight. Eat small, bland meals (nothing too taxing for the digestive system), go to bed early and try to stop children from becoming too excited. How? I don't really know, but avoid last-minute hassles, rows about who put what where, and who is the idiot who did such and such. Get to the airport in time to organise everything and everyone calmly. Walk around and look at the shops and planes; talk quietly about going on the plane and what it will be like. Try to keep everything as relaxed as possible.

Motion Sickness

Travel sickness is something which affects lots of children. The only time our children have been very sick when flying was on a short but extremely bumpy domestic flight in Australia. And by a stroke of luck we checked in rather late and had to sit three and one; luck of the toss, I got the one seat left in business class while Tony sat with the kids back in economy! Along with half of the other passengers on this flight Tashi and Kieran were both airsick! We've also had one bout of seasickness with them on an equally bumpy high speed catamaran trip out to the Great Barrier Reef.

If your children are prone to motion sickness, it's probably best to have something to hand just in case they get sick. There are certainly some trips which test anyone's equilibrium – Great Barrier Reef trips in Australia can be notoriously bumpy, flights in light aircraft over mountains can have you soaring up and down like a yo-yo and there are some equally stomach-stirring bus trips in developing countries.

Ginger is an old fashioned remedy for travel sickness which is becoming fashionable again. You can buy ginger capsules from many health food stores. It is best to use the capsules because fresh ginger, in the amounts you would require to take, could burn the throat. Take one or two capsules about an hour before you are due to fly. The amount you require will probably be something you learn through experience. Check with the health food store you buy it from that the capsule dosage will be suitable for your children's weight and age.

There are other preventative preparations available that your doctor can tell you about. Note that some of these motion sickness medicines can cause drowsiness. Also, they must be taken before you start the trip because when you start to feel sick it's too late. If it's any consolation, children seem to get over motion sickness remarkably quickly. On the reef trip Kieran threw-up his breakfast violently over the side, and an hour or two later wolfed down the biggest lunch he'd ever eaten. And kept it down on the way back.

What to Wear on the Flight

Comfort is the main consideration in deciding what to wear. Regardless of where you're going or the expected weather, cover all possibilities. You may be flying from winter to winter only to be delayed for hours en route at some height-of-the-hot-season hole with the airport air-conditioning out of operation and the temperatures soaring. You could just as likely end up shivering in a T-shirt in a freezing cold plane as it waits on the tarmac for caterers to settle a dispute.

We flew from the plains of India to Moscow in the middle of winter once, and then spent an hour standing outside the aircraft while security searched for a missing bag. Fortunately we'd been trekking in Nepal and were well equipped with down jackets but some sari-clad women on the flight looked distinctly uncomfortable. So regardless of your destination, come prepared.

A layer system of clothing works well. Tracksuits for children are a good idea with a T-shirt underneath and then a light jacket on top.

For very young children the terry vest/undershirt and pants set of underwear is a good base; it looks fine if they want to strip down, and with a tracksuit on top you are prepared for anything. With babies a sleeveless body shirt, the kind that fastens over the nappy, is comfortable for climbing around in, keeps draughts out, and you can add a T-shirt if required. The all-in-one stretch sleep suits are good for babies when the temperature drops. A woollen cardigan or sweater with a hood completes the ensemble and covers all eventualities.

If you want the children to look cute when you arrive, you can carry their 'good wear' separately, but don't put it on too soon – when you are taxiing to the terminal is time enough, as children can often foil their parents' best-laid plans.

For older children a tracksuit and T-shirt is a good idea so they can add or remove layers. Socks should always be worn if the flight is a long one as planes can get cold and feet really feel it!

Parents need to be comfortable too, and if you are travelling with small children remember that it's possible to get spectacularly dirty by the time you arrive. Sticky fingers, spilt food, regurgitated sweets, all have fewer places to go in a confined space and you will find yourself the main recipient.

Take-Off & Landing

Young children are more sensitive to the air-pressure changes as you climb or descend. It is a good idea to hand out chewy sweets or drinks at these times. Small babies will cry, which will clear their ears, but if you find this upsets you, giving them a drink will have the same effect.

If your children have colds you should always check with the doctor before flying. Make sure there is no ear infection involved. The doctor will probably advise a 'drying up' medication for the flight, and for small children who can't yet efficiently blow their noses a nasal spray may be recommended.

On a flight once in the States I had a

bad cold and my ears wouldn't clear on descent. The pain was agonising and obviously it showed on my face, because the flight attendant (thank you) took one look at me, went away, and returned minutes later with two polystyrene cups. He had wadded paper napkins, soaked in hot water, into the bases of the cups. He suggested I put one over each ear. Feeling rather ridiculous, I did as he said, and it worked! The hot air seemed to open up my blocked tubes and removed the pressure.

Time Zones

Time changes can really disorient children. They will usually be tired anyway from the plane trip and with their body clock alarm going off at odd times they can become worn out and miserable (when they are not bouncing around in the early hours of the morning making you worn out and miserable). Although you may feel like just falling into bed when you reach your destination, if it is mid-morning on your new time try to keep going for the rest of the day. By all means take it easy and don't rush off sight-seeing. Relax and wind down, but try to make your bed time an appropriate one. The more quickly you can get on to the new time, the faster you will adjust. This doesn't mean that you have to keep your children awake come what may. They will probably nap anyway, but try to keep the going-to-bed rituals (bath, pyjamas, stories, etc) until the time when they will actually be going to bed.

If we arrive when it is early morning on the new time I would aim to have the children sleep before or around midday for an hour or two, then wake them up and keep them awake until a reasonable bed time. They will then hopefully sleep through the night and be on their way to adapting to the time change within a few days. If we arrive later in the day, I would try to keep them awake, but quiet until bedtime in the hope that they will sleep through the night

For the first three nights on a new time zone, if it is radically behind or ahead of your personal time clock, it may be worthwhile sedating the children. Being over-tired for the first few days of a trip can really get you all off to a bad start.

The first time we visited Japan Kieran was two-years-old and spent the first night running around a deserted shopping centre between 2 am and 5 am with an exhausted Tony watching him. He just hadn't been able to settle in the hotel room, and being a typically tiny Japanese room he had no space to play. He wasn't about to be quiet, so finding a deserted spot to let him let off steam was our only option. It's on occasions like this that I pity sole parents!

Older children who have travelled before are at least aware of what is happening and although it is still hard to keep them awake when they really want to sleep, they are more likely to co-operate, and they can lie and read a book or listen to a tape rather than run around a shopping centre.

BUS & TRAIN

Making long trips by bus or train can be difficult with children when they've passed the tiny-baby stage and not yet arrived at the able-to-amuse-themselves stage. Older children who are crawling or toddling usually hate having to sit still and in cramped buses or trains you don't have much room for movement. Quite often the buses lurch along in such a way that you really have to hang on to your children.

If you do have to make a long trip, and there is no way you can break it up into smaller sections, all you can do is treat it like a plane trip. Make sure you have all you need readily available – drinks, snacks, books – whatever you think will work.

Throughout developing countries food and drink are sold by hawkers at stations, bus halts and on trains, but for very small children it's probably best to go prepared with all the food and drink you think they will need. The food available may not be suitable for your children, although you can often buy fruit or nuts, which are fine. In many places the meals on trains are pretty good, but it would still be good to have a supply of snacks that you know your children will like, and particularly a good supply of drinks.

Buses are often the most crowded and uncomfortable form of transport. You may have to hold your children for the entire journey, so if they are older than two it is probably worthwhile to pay for extra seats rather than to try and economise by keeping them on your knee.

However, in many countries this is unlikely to work. If you are travelling in a country or on a route where the buses are likely to be very crowded don't even bother getting extra seats for your children. There's no way your small children are going to stay on an extra seat, paid for or not, when many other people – old, pregnant or with children of their own – are standing. Three people inevitably squeeze into a space intended for two anyway and you will be no exception.

In some developing countries the buses can be surprisingly luxurious – there may be videos, toilets and even meal service as you travel. Sometimes it can be a case of technological overkill – the air-conditioning may be turned to 'arctic' or the music may be turned up to just above the threshold of pain. Air-con buses in Malaysia have been described as 'meat lockers on wheels' they're so cold. And hour after hour of screeching Indian movies on buses on the Indian subcontinent has to be some sort of inscrutable Asian torture.

In other developing countries and on

TRAVEL TIPS...

Remember the golden rule: if you are travelling with children, be prepared! Take all the food and drink you could possibly need. If you are travelling overnight make sure you take a blanket or warm clothes.

more remote routes the buses may be much more utilitarian. Remember the golden rule: if you are travelling with children, be prepared! Take all the food and drink you could possibly need. If you are travelling overnight make sure you take a blanket or warm clothes. In many places you will find the buses depart with quite amazing frequency, so you rarely have to hang around for long.

Bus trips can be a lot of fun; we've boarded local buses in Africa where we felt like we were the first white faces ever seen on that route and the welcome was a warm one.

For comfort, where there is a choice of bus or train, trains are probably a better bet. If the trip is a really long one, an overnight sleeper, if available, is always the best way to do it. Children love sleeping on trains, and small babies can at least lie down. Holding a small baby in your arms for a long period of time in hot weather is no fun for you or them.

If you do have to make a long trip, try to make sure that the next few days are spent somewhere nice and relaxing. Choose a comfortable hotel where the children can run around and enjoy themselves. Set up house for a few days, unpack the bags, frequent the same restaurants, give the children and yourselves as much time as you can manage to totally get the trip out of your system. While it may seem as though the children have forgotten all about the trip an hour after getting off the bus, the next time you reach the bus station you may find them yelling that they don't want to go. Never plan too many long journeys. Where they are unavoidable, space them as much as possible.

Older children will, of course, be bored on long bus trips, but they usually manage better for longer. Local people may talk to them, you can play all the usual 'travel games' and chat about what you are seeing to pass time. Have a treat for each hour after a certain period, even if it is only sweets or fruit, and take advantage of any stops. Always remember to make your children visit the toilet at every opportunity although kids are kids anywhere in the world and bus drivers always know what it means when you come striding up the aisle, child in hand. We've asked for unplanned pee stops all over the world!

In many developing countries you can use taxis for long-distance trips. These are always faster than buses and often not much more expensive. In Turkey they are known as *dolmus,* in the Middle East as service taxis. You also find them in some African countries, in Malaysia, and on some routes in Indonesia. Usually the principle is that they wait at a starting point (often near the bus station) until they have a full load, then off they go. Of course your family may well be a full load and often you can arrange to be taken right to your destination, not just dropped at the bus stop.

CAR

Renting a car can make life much easier for the travelling family. We've rented cars in places as widespread as the Cook Islands, Mexico, Sri Lanka, Indonesia and Kenya. Renting cars in developing countries does have a number of special rules which don't usually apply at your local Avis, Budget or Hertz agency.

Where importing cars is difficult or expensive the cars may not be the latest models or in the best mechanical condition. We've rented some decidedly tatty old VWs over the years but as long as it keeps going who's complaining? Check it over carefully though. Is there a jack and wheelbrace for example? Have they noted that both the outside mirrors have been broken off (so you don't get billed for them later)? We could have saved ourselves a lot of trouble once in Sri Lanka if we'd insisted that some of the tyres were not going to last the distance.

Don't count on having safety belts in the care you hire or being able to get infant seats. Some countries are surprisingly up to the minute in this respect but in others even if there were safety belts initially they're unlikely to be working. If you are planning to do a lot of travelling by car you may think it worth bringing a child's safety seat with you if you can work out a way of attaching it. Once in Indonesia we met a surgeon from an American hospital casualty department who was, not unexpectedly, extremely cautious about car safety. He had brought metre upon metre of safety belt and his family literally tied themselves into their vehicle!

Don't count on the rate card. In the West there may be special weekend rates or longer period rentals. In developing countries you may simply have to bargain. In some places the rate is totally open to negotiation and they will charge whatever you look like you might pay. In others they'll be quite open about it, if you want a newer car you pay more, if you're willing to take a well-worn example the rate will drop.

In some places it simply isn't worth renting a car. We rented a car once in Lima, Peru. It was fine for visiting places around the town but getting in and out of Lima was such a nightmare we wondered why we'd bothered. You can rent cars in Bangkok, Bombay or Cairo but who on earth would bother? On the other hand we met a family once who rented a car in Japan – seemingly the last place on earth a foreigner would want to be saddled with driving themselves – but it had worked amazingly well. They had got to all sorts of remote villages where public transport was difficult and hence foreign visitors few and far between.

In some places renting cars is very easy and there is a wide choice of local operators and competitive rates – Mexico, parts of Indonesia, and Kenya are good examples. In others there may be a real car shortage and you'll only get one if you book well ahead. Read up on the situation where you're going.

You don't need to drive yourself. The cost of renting a car is often far higher than hiring a driver in developing countries and in some places you simply can't rent cars to drive yourself but can easily get a car with driver.

LOCAL TRANSPORT

Within cities, towns and villages there is a wide choice of transport – depending on where you're going you may come across buses, taxis, auto-rickshaws, horse carriages, bicycle-rickshaws or end up walking!

In Asia children usually love bicycle-rickshaws. They're a good, cheap way to get around and rickshaw wallahs usually like children – after all they're easier to pedal around than adults! Auto-rickshaws are small, noisy, uncomfortable three-wheeler devices powered by smelly two-stroke engines. You find them in parts of Indonesia, on the Indian subcontinent and in Thailand, where they are known as *samlors* (Thai for 'three wheels') or *tuk-tuks*. Indonesian *bemos* and *colts*, Papua New Guinean PMVs, Thai *songthaews*, Kenyan *matatus* are all other forms of transport you may come across.

BICYCLE

In many places in Asia, particularly on the Indian subcontinent or in China, bicycles are easily available in touristed areas and are a good, fun way to get around. Unfortunately you won't often find children's bicycle seats available, but if you're staying somewhere for a while you could get one made. We stayed in Kathmandu for a while once, sought out the cane furniture making area and had cane bicycle seats made up, which we tied on to the rear carriers of our rented bikes. We managed to sell them to other travelling parents when we left.

WALKING & TREKKING

Trekking has increased dramatically in popularity, particularly in Nepal where many trekking companies offer family treks. These are generally very well organised and able to deal with quite small children, though they usually have an age limit. Trekking on your own in Nepal with your children is also possible, if you take into consideration your children's and your own needs when planning the trip. With small children don't plan to go too high or too far. No matter how experienced a walker you are, very young children do not acclimatise to high altitudes as easily as adults and serious problems can result. Altitude sickness can be fatal and even a minor case should be taken seriously.

There are many walks in Nepal which are suited to children of all ages. You can hire porters who will carry your packs and your children, and there are many books and agencies available that can give you advice. In Kathmandu and Pokhara trekking shops and agencies abound, and they can put you on the right track for hiring porters. With small children who are not yet walking, you have to carry the usual equipment. In many areas of Nepal it is not necessary to carry a tent and camping gear as all along the route there are hotels, tea houses and restaurants where you can stay and eat. But it is a good idea to carry your own sleeping bags and a container for water.

Older children, from crawlers to toddlers, may be carried most of the way, but do give them time to do whatever it is they are doing, whether it be crawling in the grass for a while beside the track or toddling along the path by themselves – it is a trip for them too, and they need to get their turn.

Children who are walking may get bored and want to be carried a lot. Children always enjoy it more when there are other kids their own age around, so it may be a good idea to try to organise a trek with other families.

We organised a trek in Nepal for several friends and their children. The oldest child was 12-years-old, the youngest was six. We had a wonderful time: we walked for eight days and some of it was pretty daunting, however all the children managed it really well, and later said it was the best holiday ever. We had porters to carry our bags, and the full trekking contingent, cook, guide, tents etc. The trekking company we booked with even sent along some Nepalese children who spoke a little English and two Nepalese teenagers to help look after them all. Our kids learnt to count in Nepalese, sing songs and every night they played riotous games together. It was a truly great trip.

You need to protect yourselves against the elements – sun, cold, etc – and carry lots of snacks and drinks with you. In cooler weather blanket sleepers make good walking clothes for small children. Add a hood, mittens and a sleeveless jacket and the child is cosy from head to food, and comfortable. If you are planning a cold-weather trek make sure the child's shoes will fit over the plastic 'feet' in the blanket sleeper. Shoes should be comfortable over warm socks. Many experienced walkers recommend tennis shoes or slip-on rubber boots with felt inner soles.

Most children like to carry their own packs. These don't have to be expensive, but do have to be light and easy to carry. Children from three years of age can carry their own but there will certainly be some passing it on to the accompanying adults. Check that there are no uncomfortable lumps, let them carry their own snacks and drinks, a flashlight and one or two favourite toys.

The half-length sleeping bags used by climbers are ideal for children to use and much better quality than the average child size sleeping bag, although the latter are probably fine for warm-weather trekking.

If you haven't hired a porter to carry your children, be prepared to do the carrying for a fair proportion of the trip as children tire easily. Obviously for babies and young children a backpack or similar carrier will be essential, while older but still portable children may ride comfortably on their parent's shoulders or back. However, this soon becomes uncomfortable for the parent, and on rocky, steep or uneven surfaces it can become difficult and unsafe.

Don't try to cover as much ground as you would without children. This sounds obvious, but you would be surprised how often parents overlook the obvious. Lots of rest stops are necessary, and bear in mind, too, that during the rest stops you

TRAVEL TIPS...

Dress your children in brightly coloured clothes so they are always easy to spot, and pin a whistle to their jacket, so they can signal you if necessary.

will have to keep working – entertaining, feeding, washing, whatever. Children are a never-ending source of things to do! Always carry an extra set of clothes in an easily accessible spot. Even amongst the mountains children will be able to find the one puddle of water or mud hole for miles around.

Dress your children in brightly coloured clothes so they are always easy to spot, and pin a whistle to their jacket, so they can signal you if necessary.

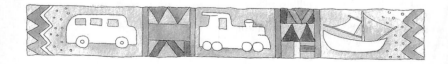

USA & NEPAL

Tashi Wheeler has been travelling with her parents since she was a baby. She is now 14 years old.

I HAVE BEEN TRAVELLING SINCE I WAS EIGHT-MONTHS-OLD, and I'm now four-teen-years-old. It's been great and I've really enjoyed going away each holiday and spending time in different countries and meeting all sorts of people. Of course I don't remember everything from each trip, but I remember enough to tell people what we've done.

One trip that I remember really well was when we drove from one side of America to the other in a 1959 cadillac Coupe de Ville. We started in California and ended up in Boston and saw all the different states along the way.

One place I really enjoyed on that trip was Las Vegas. OK, so my parents and other adults think it's tack'o'rama, and maybe it is, but it was really fun. It felt like being a tiny ant living in Disneyland with the huge castle, sphinx and so on all around you. I could have spent all day going from hotel to hotel to see the special effects and watch each of them over and over again. At the Mirage, where we were staying, a huge underwater volcano erupted out the front every fifteen minutes. At the Excalibur the magician Merlin came out of a castle and used his magic to send a ginormous fire-breathing dragon (around 60 million times the size of my house) back under the hotel.

In Phoenix we went to a basketball game between the Phoenix Suns and the Denver Nuggets. The Suns thrashed the Nuggets. For me, it was just as interesting to watch the 'Cube' screen that hung above the middle of the court with cartoons of the players etc, as it was to watch the game. Not so for my brother who was screaming and yelling for his team and concentrating hard on the game. He's a real basketball fan!

Let's leave America and travel to Nepal, the home of the Himalayas. This is

one of my favourite countries and we go back there every two or three years. We've been trekking there twice. When I was around eight-years-old I went with my family and no one else. It was really fun. One day we stopped off in a village and our cook bought two live chickens. I really wanted to carry the rooster so I asked if I could. The cook grudgingly said 'yes', so I carried the rooster and my brother carried the hen. Mum and Dad did try and tell us that we were meant to be eating them that night and although I knew it was true I didn't think they'd actually kill them. Didn't I get a surprise when we reached our campsite at the top of the hill and the cook whipped the chickens away and cut their heads off. Although I was upset, they made a nice curry for dinner.

The second time we went trekking in Nepal was with all our friends, when we did the Helambu trek. Apart from trekking, we would go around the markets and little shops and stalls where they sold all sorts of stuff; from household appliances, clothing and cloth, to jewellery. They had beautiful rings and coloured bangles made of shiny metals in different sizes. I used to sit in a little shop and bargain with the women over what was a fair price for thirty jade-green glass bangles.

Although I love travelling, a few holidays at home wouldn't hurt. Sometimes I think I'm missing out on stuff by being away from home during the holidays. Sometimes you feel left out when you get back to school and your friends are talking about the great time they had when they went to the beach together. It can hurt if they start closing you out.

If you do travel you can go back to school and boast about what you'd done overseas. I've had my hair plaited in the Carribean, in Egypt I rode a camel around the pyramids, and I rode a beautiful Arabian horse around the sphinxes. You can also get a great tan in the middle of winter.

Because travelling is part of my parents' job by the time I move out of home I'll have already seen the world. Maybe I'll do something in travel too when I'm older: I don't think I'd be happy to stay in Australia without travelling. Australia's a beautiful country but travelling is like a drug: it's hard to stop once you've started. It's kind of addictive and makes you want to try new places and different things.

travel stories

I love riding on aeroplanes; it's strange to think of yourself so far above the ground, moving so quickly, when you don't feel like you're moving anywhere. I always take a really good book and my walkman on flights. My brother can sit and play gameboy for hours and the little travel games are good. When we were younger we used to be given Activity books. Bring some of your own colouring-in books and sticker books.

> *'...even my parents who live off aeroplane food for half the year know that children's meals are much, much, much nicer than what they're given. '*

And there's always the meals. If you take children anywhere by plane make sure you do one thing for them: order children's meals. They're so much nicer; even my parents who live off aeroplane food for half the year know that children's meals are much, much, much nicer than what they're given. All you have to do is say how many you'd like when you book your tickets.

Tashi Wheeler

OUTBACK AUSTRALIA

*Hugh Finlay,
Linda Henderson
(pictured with Vera)
and daughters
Ella (4½) and
Vera (one) travelled
by car through
outback Australia.*

A USTRALIA IS A BIG PLACE – a bloody big place – and unless you have unlimited funds, getting around it, with or without kids, generally means travelling by road. In 1993, Linda and I packed our two daughters, Ella and Vera (then aged 4½ and one-year-old respectively), into the LP 4WD for an update trip to the Northern Territory.

It was obvious before we even started that boredom was going to be the main problem with the kids. Sure, the Australian countryside is picturesque and full of interest, but there's a hell of a lot of it, and it can be a long time between drinks. Once you're into the outback, a strip of black or dusty road heading arrow-straight to the horizon is often all that breaks up the monotony of endless km of scrub or desert either side.

For Ella the main distraction was a personal cassette player; there was no way I was going to listen to Play School songs and kids' stories for hours – and days – on end. It was an excellent way to keep her amused; she'd put the headphones on and slip into a state of suspended animation while she listened for hours. Occasionally she was so absorbed we had trouble coaxing her from the vehicle when we stopped for a break.

Being much younger, Vera was harder to amuse – she got an awful lot of sleep during the trip! Each day when we were travelling one of us would spend a few hours in the back seat, between the two girls, and try various activities to keep them occupied – card and board games, 'I Spy', story books and drawing all helped to pass the time.

The ideal way to do a trip such as this is to only spend about four hours in the car each day. Unfortunately with the distances we had to cover we invariably

travel stories

spent up to eight hours driving, which was pretty tough on the kids – long periods of forced physical confinement are not conducive to family harmony!

The long hours spent in the car were the downside, but this was more than offset by the amazing places we would get to at the end. One of the highlights of the trip was the Witjira National Park on the edge of the Simpson Desert in the far north of South Australia. We arrived late one afternoon at the Dalhousie Hot Springs, literally an oasis in the desert. The day's driving had been much longer than planned, but the promise of a swim at the end limited the whines of 'When are we *ever* going to get there?' which inevitably came from the back seat as the day wore on, seemingly without end as far as the kids were concerned. The joy for all of us at being able to have a swim – albeit a very warm one – after a long day and in such amazing surroundings was hard to match.

> **' Few people would argue that cooping your-self up in a bumpy tin box for hours on end with a couple of young kids is a non-stop barrel of laughs... '**

Most nights we were camping or simply sleeping out under the stars. Fortunately our kids are among the majority who find camping a great adventure. We were totally self-sufficient and so were able to bush camp in some remote places with no-one else for miles around. One such place was Boggy Hole, an unflattering name for a beautiful billabong on the (mostly dry) Finke River in central Australia. We relaxed and enjoyed the surroundings, the kids found the mud... Only a day's drive from here is one of the busiest and best equipped campsites in the outback – at Uluru – where you can pitch your tent on a patch of immaculately maintained, *green*, prickle-free lawn, dine in air-conditioned comfort, keep the desert at arm's length and a cold beer in arm's reach!

No account of travel in Australia, especially the outback, would be complete without a whinge about the flies! At certain times of the year these little bastards are diabolical! Our trip was at the end of winter, so the flies were getting worse by the day. Initially we came across people wearing their cheap and nasty 'Genuine Ausie (sic) Fly Net' (made in Taiwan), and thought they were a bunch of fairies. No self-respecting visitor to the outback would be seen dead in one, or so we thought. Before long we'd swallowed our pride (along with numerous flies), bought our own and were grateful that someone had had the foresight to import them.

travel stories

While there are plenty of places in Australia which would have been much easier to visit, few would offer the challenges of the outback. As always, travelling with children adds another dimension to that challenge. Few people would argue that cooping yourself up in a bumpy tin box for hours on end with a couple of young kids is a non-stop barrel of laughs, but as long as you can maintain a sense of humour and preserve a modicum of sanity, it can be wonderfully rewarding for all.

Hugh Finlay

BRAZIL

Gabriela Draffen (four) travelled to Brazil with her parents Stella & Andrew, and baby brother Christopher.

BRAZILIANS DELIGHT IN THEIR CHILDREN. They love to spoil their macho heirs and treat their daughters as princesas. Our daughter, Gabriela, a lively four-year-old, was getting the 'princess' treatment in Sao Paulo, so she wasn't very happy to leave. She was enjoying the visits to family and friends; riding in the lifts to their apartments was a novelty for her. And at the Sunday Market at Praca Republica in the centre of town there was plenty of things for kids to see – like a fortune-telling parrot, and toy-hawkers twirling wind-up plastic fish in small tubs of water.

We decided to travel from Sao Paulo to Rio de Janeiro via the coast road, a distance of some 550km. The plan was to take five or six days, stopping off at a couple of places on the way before spending a few days in Rio. Most people imagine Brazil as a destination for adventurous solo travellers, which is true. But the South and South-East are well-developed regions, with an excellent road and bus system, so it's easy for families to travel. We opted for a few short bus rides of two to three hours a time. It seemed a better idea to spend more money on hotels.

We left Sao Paulo one morning, taking the metro to the main bus terminal. We all carried small daypacks, as the weather was good and we only needed shirts and shorts for the whole time. When you're travelling with kids on the Brazilian coast the essentials are: sunscreen, hats, a fan in the room, mosquito nets, and plenty of running water.

A three-hour trip on a modern bus took us to Sao Sebastiao, a small town on the coast. Since it was mid-week, we hadn't bothered to book into any hotels, choosing instead to wander around a bit when we got there and then have some lunch. Gabriela, like most Brazilians, enjoys a meal of rice, beans, *farinha* (manioc flour) and fresh fish. And since it's customary to mix the rice and beans with the *farinha*, 'playing with your food' is an obvious attraction. It's not spicy either, so most kids enjoy it and adults can always add some chilli if they need a bit more heat.

However, lunch usually consisted of a snack at the beach. Gabriela couldn't get enough. Her favourites were *milho* (corn on a stick), *pasteis* (deep fried pastries containing either mince beef or cheese) and icy poles made from real fruit. All washed down with coconut milk straight from the nut. The vendors keep the coconuts on ice – beautiful.

> **' Being only a month before Carnival, the local samba bands were practising a lot. '**

We travelled slowly for the next few days. At each town we followed the same pattern: a leisurely breakfast, off to the beach, lunch at the beach and then back to the hotel for a siesta. By around 9 pm we were ready to go out again, wandering around the beachfront or the town, stopping for a bite to eat or a larger meal if we were hungry.

Then we looked for the music. there's always some live music going on. Being only a month before Carnival, the local samba bands were practising a lot. And they're easy to find! There were rows of girls Gabriela's age dancing. She couldn't quite match their speed; she slept extremely well at night after trying to keep up!

Christo Redentor statue, Rio de Janeiro

travel stories

Even though we only stayed in Rio for a couple of days, we had a great time. Highlights for Gabriela were the trip in the cable-car to the top of the Sugarloaf, and the cog-railway up Corcovado to see the huge statue of Christ that overlooks the city. Afternoons we spent at the beach.

The beach in Rio is a circus. There's always something going on because for *cariocas* (natives of Rio) it's their backyard. There are vendors selling everything from suntan lotion to cold tea. All of them use different noisemakers so you know they're in the area. Kids will love it, but keep a close eye on them near the water, because it gets deep after a few steps, and there are some strong undertows.

For the return trip, we took the night train from Rio, arriving in Sao Paulo the next morning. The old Pullman railway cars, with their fold-up washbasins, fold-down bunk and miniature fans, kept Gabriela busy for ages.

I got the feeling she couldn't have cared less about the scenery in Rio, one of the most beautiful cities in the world. The means of transport always seemed to be the main attraction.

Andrew Draffen

MALAYSIA

*Hugh Finlay &
Linda Henderson
spent a month
in Peninsular
Malaysia with their
daughter Ella, aged
16 months (pictured
here as Malaysian
goddess).*

ELLA WAS 16-MONTHS-OLD when Linda and I first decided to take her travelling – a six-week trip to Peninsular Malaysia. We ignored the usual helpful and encouraging tips – such as: 'You're bloody mad!' – proffered by friends and relatives, and headed for the airport. As this was our first trip with an infant, we had yet to learn the art of minimal packing – we'd managed to leave the kitchen sink behind, but seemed to have everything else, including Ella's stroller, and car safety seat (as we intended hiring a car for the bulk of our first family trip).

We landed in Singapore, and headed almost immediately across the causeway to Johor Bahru in Malaysia, where we picked up the rental car. Our first problem arose when we went to fit Ella's car seat into the back of the car – no rear seat belts. It did fit into the front OK, but this then left one of us unrestrained in the rear. While this doesn't seem of great concern to the locals, who happily cram themselves in, it definitely was of concern to us, especially after seeing the overtaking tactics of some of the drivers on our first day on the road.

The problem was solved in a way the rental company might not have been overjoyed about. I pulled out my 10 mm spanner (as I said, we packed everything!) and had the back seat out in a flash. We then used a length of rope to tie the child seat to the car seat, and then refitted the whole thing back into the car. The end result was less than pretty, with ropes going all over the place, but at least we were all strapped in.

Once on the road – in our slightly modified vehicle – everything was fine. Renting your own transport is, of course, expensive, but it is also one of the biggest single steps you can take towards making life on the road with kids easy

– or at least easier. While you certainly miss some of the local colour that public transport provides, you also miss the heat, crowds, delays, and long hours in often cramped conditions too! In our case it also meant we were able to travel in air-conditioned comfort, and surround ourselves with even more gear...

> ‘ *...the one incident which sticks vividly in my mind is Ella's strawberry yoghurt projectile vomit in the back of the car...* ’

Travelling up the west coast of the peninsula was a breeze – pretty good roads, cheap and clean hotels, plenty of child-friendly restaurants (high chairs, washable floors – and walls – bomb-proof plastic crockery and unflappable staff) and people who treated kids like human beings – albeit ones which should be poked, stroked, cooed at and fussed over at every possible opportunity – rather than some nasty affliction which only careless people got themselves mixed up with. While the trip was basically trouble free, the one incident which sticks vividly in my mind is Ella's strawberry yoghurt projectile vomit in the back of the car, but I'll spare you the details!

Our final destination was Penang, where we handed back the car *(sans* rope and car seat and only slightly soiled!) and returned ourselves to the ranks of car-less travellers. We flew to the small resort island of Langkawi in the far north, which has beaches even Australians would call good, for a few days rest before our flight home. It was the second island we'd visited (Pangkor, south-west of Kuala Lumpur being the other), and although quite developed, was still sufficiently low-key to be cheap and pleasant.

On Langkawi the main form of transport is motorbike. Having closely observed the local habit of putting three or more on a motorbike, we decided to do the same as the roads were good and the traffic negligible. In retrospect it was probably a pretty silly thing to do; at the time it was great, and we were able to visit many places which would have been inaccessible otherwise.

On the whole Malaysia is an excellent destination for travel with children, especially if it is your first trip with young ones in tow.

Hugh Finlay

ON THE ROAD

RULES OF THE ROAD
Long-Distance Travel

Some children may love all-day bus trips, or three-day train journeys through India, or visiting museums and art galleries for hours on end, but I wouldn't count on being the parent of such children.

Many children, however, will enjoy all of these things in child-sized doses. There are occasions when an all-day bus trip is necessary and an overnight trip on a train with a sleeper may be very exciting, but three days on a train tests anybody's endurance level, so maybe the Trans-Siberian journey should wait until your children are old enough to decide that this is how they want to spend their vacation.

Visiting Museums & Other Sights

Museums can be fascinating, as can ruined cities and ancient buildings: Tashi and Kieran thought Macchu Picchu was great – a terrific place for a game of hide and seek! The superb Anthropological Museum in Mexico City may have limited appeal to children, but the fountains and pond outside kept them happy for quite a while, while we browsed. Most things you want to do will have some appeal for children, if not in quite the way you thought.

Taking Turns

With very young children you may decide you would enjoy a gallery visit more if you went solo, so parents can split up; one stays with the child and one visits the museum, and next day vice-versa. Some travelling parents take it in turns to have one day off each week. This may be the day when you wander around, stopping for cold drinks or snacks wherever takes your fancy, browsing through shops or talking to other travellers, or just lazing on the beach reading a book, savouring the fact that there are no interruptions. Some people find this works very well, giving each parent a safety valve.

When your children are a bit older they may well accept the 'turns' system. You explain to them that you want to visit a museum in the morning, but in the afternoon they get to choose what they want to do, whether it is playing in their room, shopping for presents for friends, going to a playground or swimming pool or whatever. If you do have a day on a bus, make the next day a rest day, when you all relax and the children get to choose the activities.

Tiredness

Young children get very tired and, like everyone else, cope less well with life when they are. Avoiding overtiring your

TRAVEL TIPS...

Don't fill your days with things to do; children need some unstructured playtime in each day.

children is easier said than done, but try to structure your day around their needs. Think about what you want to do and then how best to do it. If it is a long bus trip to your destination, the morning may be the best time to go, when the children are fresh and cheerful, and the ride back may be a good time for them to have a sleep. Children rarely do things to plan, but knowing your children will give you some clues on how to structure things.

Don't fill your days with things to do; children need some unstructured playtime in each day. Take a couple of hours each day to retire to your hotel and let them put in a few hours as they please – whether it is playing with toys, drawing, reading, being read to or whatever.

Space to Play

Where possible, choose places to stay with your children in mind. Any kind of garden, verandah or space near your room that is safe, is worth having. A swimming pool is top of the desirable facilities: my two can spend hours jumping in and splashing around and

after a hot sticky morning of sightseeing it seems like heaven. A hotel room in itself is not a very stimulating environment, but being able to sit on a verandah and watch people going about their business, or run around a small patch of garden chasing a butterfly, may just be the difference between being able to relax and let go for a while and feeling trapped and frustrated. At one hotel in Bali, Tashi became very friendly with the gardener and used to follow him around 'helping' with his work; she loved it and he seemed pleased by her devotion.

Children's Experiences

Allow your children to experience things in their own way. The Buddha statue may seem very impressive to you, but if your son seems to be more interested in the vendor of sticky drinks, don't think the trip is a failure and your little philistine would have been better at home. You'll be surprised at the memories he will take home, and often quite unprepared for the insights he will have of the culture and people he met.

Don't devalue the things your children find exciting and wonderful or try to always turn their attention to what you feel is a more important aspect of what you are seeing. As long as they find something exciting and wonderful the trip will be a success.

Children's Activities

Just about everywhere you can find things that seem to be tailor-made for children. They will be fascinated by the obvious differences from life at home – the houses, the different forms of transport (horse carts, rickshaws, crowded buses, whatever), the way people dress and the local customs. There are also special things which are especially thrilling for children: the elephant school in Thailand, kite flying on the east coast of Malaysia, the bat cave in Bali, and wildlife almost anywhere.

Equally, there are things that adults might pass by which prove absolutely irresistible to children. We visited a small-town fun fair in Ecuador that may have paled beside Santa Cruz or Luna Park but was just fine for two small kids. Dunia Fantasi in Jakarta, a pretty good attempt at a sort of Asian Disneyland, was one of the high spots of a visit to Java. The Tiger Balm gardens in Singapore and Hong Kong are deliciously terrifying and markets are generally pretty exciting wherever they are.

There are plenty of special attractions for children all over the world and it's fascinating to see how they are often much the same as back home. We've tried out local playgrounds from India to Ecuador or Bolivia to Zimbabwe: a visit to the numerous temples in Japan's temple city of Kyoto was interspersed with trying out the slides and swings in tiny playgrounds. One thing to take into consideration is the fact that in third-world countries zoos, aquariums etc are often sad places where animals are treated disgracefully. It may be wise to avoid such sights unless you have reliable information that they are pleasant places to visit.

Besides all the special treats and children's attractions, don't underestimate their ability to be awed, enchanted and delighted by more 'cultural' pursuits.

Stories of the legends behind the temple sculptures, the rituals enacted each day at religious ceremonies, and the local festivals can all be explained simply – even to a very young child.

On a visit to Kathmandu our early morning walk to breakfast was always full of excitement and interest. We saw the markets being set up, the man spinning clay into little *chai* (tea) cups, a cow stealing vegetables from a stall, all before our morning bowl of muesli! Tashi was also most impressed by Kathmandu's Kala (Black) Bhairab statue. We were told that naughty children were taken here and shown this fearsome statue of Shiva to encourage them to reform. Tashi was certainly thoughtful after hearing this story and seeing the fearful six-arm figure!

Involving your Children

While you are travelling, keep your children informed of your plans. Tell them where you are going, what you want to see, how you will get there, how long it will take – all the details. Not only will your children find this interesting but it helps to give them a sense of security. Help them choose postcards to send back, even if you do the writing.

Let them have some local money and encourage them to make transactions at the market (with you overseeing of course). In countries like India and Nepal, markets have stall after stall selling brightly coloured, plastic bangles, necklaces and wonderful hair ornaments which will totally delight most little girls. Buy some for their friends back home.

In Africa, Kieran became hooked on the concept of bargaining and would wander through the markets trying to unload unwanted possessions for a much more interesting carving. The stall holders were usually so tickled at his cheek that he never came away empty handed! Once on a bus he entertained a large group of hawkers with his sales pitch in a desperate attempt to own a Maasai shield!

When walking through the streets of Cuzco, in Peru, we were often taken aback at how much Tashi noticed for herself, and how much we could talk to her about what we were seeing. Don't assume that some things are not interesting to your children because of their age. Your children will be interested in almost everything, given the chance. But keep it all in moderation; if you march them around while you spout information and act like a school teacher on a 'cultural' trip you may well just turn them off.

Statues are interesting anywhere and make great climbing frames, but be aware of cultural sensitivities: you should *never* let your children climb on Buddha statues. Even temples and buildings can be made to seem interesting if you have a little bit of knowledge of their history or architecture.

This all means that you have to be prepared yourself. You don't have to know everything – dates and architectural styles are not what children are interested in – but the stories and legends associated with historical buildings, monuments and statues will interest them. Take the time and trouble to understand why people are doing what they are doing. If your children ask and you don't know, find out from a book or ask someone who does.

As your children get older you will probably find yourselves discussing politics, social issues, moral concerns and even justifying your role as tourist. Hopefully this means that you have done your job well and used travelling as a way to educate your children and encourage them to ask questions. Bear this in mind if you can as you find yourself embroiled in an endless, unwinnable argument with well-travelled and very righteous teenagers!

Expectations

Away from our familiar environment things aren't always quite what you expect. A glass-bottom boat trip to view the coral in Sri Lanka turned out to be hanging over the edge of a dugout canoe to look into a glass-bottomed box. I sat perched on the edge of the canoe, feet trailing in the water with a worried eight-month-old Kieran clutching me. Although the experience turned out to be different to what we thought it would be, if you can be flexible and take some chances you'll make the most of travel.

PLACES TO STAY
Settling In

Some children will sleep anywhere with a minimum of fuss. At one stage my children certainly did not fit into that category, although they are much better sleepers now they are older. If your children are members of the great non-sleepers conspiracy there are a number of possible solutions.

TRAVEL TIPS...

...make sure you are always settled into the hotel early in the afternoon to give your children time to get used to the room.

Your children may not take to too much moving around. You may find that they find it hard to settle in a new room. It is worthwhile to make sure you are always settled into the hotel early in the afternoon to give your children time to get used to the room. Even very young babies can be extremely sensitive to their surroundings. Try to give them time to explore the room, play in it, learn where the bathroom is, etc. It is also an idea to carry something personal which will make the room familiar. Try to have something that a baby can always have within view; a small hanging object, a fluffy toy that sits on the bed, a familiar rug or cuddly will help children settle.

Let older children play house. They can set out their toys and books and choose a drawer or space to put their clothes in. Little boys and girls love to bustle around 'tidying up' and each new room can provide an excellent opportunity. If they want to move things, let them (within reason).

Sleep

The fact that you are all sleeping in the same room may also be unsettling for your children. I find that the younger they are, the more difficult it is. Tashi will now sleep through anything, yet as a baby the slightest noise would have her awake and noisy. Babies tend to sleep lightly and are easily disturbed.

Getting children to have daytime naps can also be a problem on the road. Small children need a sleep during the day and will be extra tired when travelling. Some children may sleep quite happily on your shoulder wherever you may be, others need to be laid down on a bed, given a drink and a cuddle before they can drift off.

When Tashi was two-years-old we spent an hour or so every afternoon lying beside her telling stories and singing songs before she would go to sleep. You can sometimes make a choice: keep your children awake all afternoon, and put them to bed early (which means your day ends early too); or insist that they have an afternoon nap in the hope and you can all go out to eat at night without exhaustion making the experience a misery for all of you.

When I say you have a choice, I am assuming your children will comply – they don't always. It was always a battle to get Tashi to sleep and from the day she was born sleep was something she tried to do without. When she was 18-months-old she gave up all daytime naps but got into the habit of going to bed at 6 to 6.30 pm and sleeping a straight 12 hours. When she was little we stuck to that routine when travelling and it worked quite well. From the age of two, however, we found that the travelling and the heat tired her out, so that we could get her to go to sleep in the afternoon (with songs, etc!) and she would stay up quite late, quite happily.

Kieran however, was quite a different kettle of fish. He would sleep until midnight, after which he would wake for a chat at least once before dawn. He liked to have a good morning sleep, in a bed, and then until he was 13-months-old, again in the afternoon. Which meant that our days had to be structured around his naps. This was sometimes awkward, and at times he just had to accept that bed was not available, but on the whole we tried to keep to the routine he liked. On his first trip, when he was just four-months-old and he was more able to sleep anywhere, we took a reclining stroller and he would sleep in that. However, where possible, we did try to organise things to suit him.

As he got older it was more difficult; no matter how tired he got, if he couldn't lie down and have a sleep, he was miserable and quite able to keep himself awake way beyond the point where he could cope. It is not worth trying to force your children to 'get used to it' in this sort of situation; you will simply have to organise your travelling to suit them. This is where the compromise comes in – you have to, your children won't.

Older children are much easier; they usually like new hotel rooms, and will run around checking out what they offer. Usually they have a preferred bed to sleep on within minutes of entering the room, and they also like to set out their toys and books and make a space for themselves. Going to bed at night is the usual matter of getting them to settle down, but they usually present few problems as the days' events will have worn them out.

When there are four of you it may be easier to take two rooms side by side, rather than all pile into one. In some places, like Bali, you can often get two rooms sharing a verandah, and this can quickly assume a very homelike atmosphere, with the verandah becoming your private 'sitting room'. You also have the benefit of two bathrooms. It's surprising how often even pretty basic hotels have some sort of family room or 'suite'. Getting a place where you have your space and the children have theirs can make a real difference to everybody's comfort.

With a verandah or some separate space the parents can sit and read or talk while the children eventually go to sleep. Sometimes this is not possible, so you are stuck with trying to dim the room sufficiently to encourage the children to sleep but not so much that you are forced to go to bed too. As the children get older you may find that they can stay awake until reasonably late, and then you can all go to bed at the same time.

Cots

Expensive 'international standard' hotels can almost always supply them and in many places even more reasonably priced hotels will have something for a baby or small child to sleep in. Some places will charge more for a cot but many cheap places will not have heard of them; in developing countries even many medium-priced hotels will look at you with incomprehension.

I didn't carry a port-a-cot with me for either of the children, and although it would have been useful at times we managed without one. There are all sorts of alternatives, including the children simply sleeping with you, although if your children are restless sleepers, like Tashi was, that can be no fun at all.

Two armchairs placed facing each other can make a fine, safe sleeping cot for a small child. Even if you don't leave them there all night it can be useful for daytime sleeps, and for the first part of the evening when the baby is asleep, but the rest of you are sitting up reading or whatever. A large drawer might also prove serviceable as an improvised cot.

From 18-months-old onwards children (depending on how big they are and how confident) can really go into a bed. You can always make sure they get a bed against the wall and put a pillow beside them if you worry about them falling out.

Bathing

Bathing your children may sound very simple but, depending on the age of your child, it may require some organisation, particularly if you are travelling on a budget or off the beaten track and your room does not have an attached bathroom, or there is no bathtub in the bathroom. Sometimes, as in Indonesia, even a Western-type shower may not be available. Most children under 12-months-old are not quite ready for an Indonesian *mandi* – standing in the bathroom sloshing buckets of cold water over their heads. You can often ask for hot water to bathe a small child in but it can take some time to produce and in tropical areas where nobody washes in hot water you will be looked at somewhat askance! The hotel may also have a tin bath, or a plastic basin you can borrow.

One place we stayed at in Pokhara, Nepal, had two plastic basins for washing clothes. I bathed Tashi and Kieran on the grass outside during the hottest part of the day (because the water was cold) by sitting them in one basin each and scrubbing them down. They thought it was great fun. Tashi at two-years-old thought Indonesian *mandis* were great, but her feet were the only part of her that really got washed. Now both children love them and have great fun hurling water around and shrieking with pleasure. Staying in *ryokan*, the traditional Japanese inns, the children enjoyed following the local custom: you wash outside the bath, then sit and soak in the hot water.

Some small children will take showers, but most of them do not like the experience of water gushing down on them. When Kieran was really little, I used to just lie him on the plastic change mat I had brought, get a bucket of warmish water and wash him down with a cloth. Even in the tropics it can get very cool when the sun goes down (or at least comparatively cooler) and the children may complain loudly about the cold water, so try and wash them while the day is still pretty warm. Then you can let them splash around as much as they like and hopefully clean them in the process.

Occasionally you will strike it lucky and find a bathroom with a tub, not just a shower. While this is a great distraction for most kids, you need to make sure that they don't drink from the water, something which they may be used to doing at home (whether you're aware of it or not!).

For teeth cleaning, keep bottled or boiled, purified water in the bathroom and make sure your children know that it must be used when cleaning teeth and for rinsing the toothbrush. Small children often swallow quite a lot of water when cleaning their teeth, so although you may not think it is necessary for yourself, try to make it a rule for the children, and don't let them see you doing otherwise.

Toilets

If your children are past the nappy stage, they may well be at the 'toilet-fixation' stage. You know, when they can't pass up the opportunity to use a different toilet wherever they go? I remember having to swiftly curtail Tashi's delight at being let loose in a showroom full of new bathroom fittings. With both our children there was a phase where no restaurant visit (or flight for that matter) was complete without a thorough inspection of the sanitary facilities.

If, however, toilet facilities are not conveniently to hand and your child gets caught short, any restaurant, coffee shop or hotel will let you use their bathrooms in an emergency, whether you are a patron or not. In small towns or villages, if there is an absence of public places, you can always explain the situation to a pleasant looking bystander (you will almost always have an entourage around you). Whether or not you will always want to use the facilities offered, is another ques-

tion. If you are absolutely stuck, do what the locals do, hold your child out over a drain, or any other likely place.

In parts of Asia where toilets are usually of the squat down rather than familiar, Western sit-up variety your children may baulk at these 'hole in the ground' affairs. Try to be patient, I'll bet you had reservations too when you first saw them. If you show them how it's done, they'll probably come to regard it at least as an interesting novelty. Always go with them and help them to get organised – they will probably want to be held while they are squatting; many children are afraid they are about to disappear down the hole.

PLACES TO EAT

Even in the most remote places small local restaurants will be quite happy to see children. Even the open-air stall in a small town in Malaysia will have a high chair which proprietors will produce with a flourish when they see you coming. In fact in some developing countries they will do everything other than actually feed your child. I don't know how many times Tashi or Kieran were taken away for a walk to see the relatives while I ate my meal in peace.

Nor do most small places mind the mess; lots of little street-front restaurants in Asia have concrete floors which brush straight on to the street. Besides, what self-respecting Chinese would expect anyone to eat without making a mess?

Nevertheless, you may find that you have to eat at more expensive restaurants or in the more expensive hotels more often than you might wish. Small children are notoriously unadventurous in their eating habits and you may have to pass up some wonderful local eating opportunities while you search for some place that can produce an imitation of a mundane cheese and tomato sandwich or a hot dog. Having said that, beware of the hot dogs that look wonderful but with the first bite bring a howl of pained disbelief because the 'tomato sauce' is really chilli, and the 'spaghetti bolognese' that bears no earthly resemblance in taste to what your children (and you) are used to. No matter how they are described on the menu you will to some extent just have to cross your fingers and hope. A quick rule of thumb is the bigger and flashier the hotel, the more 'authentic' the Western food will be.

Unfamiliar food or not, there are some great dining possibilities which children will love. In Japan eating out is made much easier by the plastic versions of what you can expect to eat inside, displayed in the window of the restaurant. While it certainly makes ordering easy you may have to dissuade your child from ordering the most luridly coloured dishes. Remind them they have to eat them as well as look at them!

One seafood restaurant we visited several times in Sri Lanka provided endless interest with its corral of crabs, awaiting their fate. In Singapore and in other parts of Asia many Chinese restaurants have virtual aquariums of fish, prawns and other extremely fresh dining possibilities. The chef spinning out noodles on the spot had our kids enthralled at a restaurant in Hong Kong and what child could resist a Mongolian hot pot, Korean barbecue or Malaysian steamboat where you cook the food yourself, Swiss fondue style, right on the table. While all this may be fun, the children may still not eat.

We've had some wonderful children's food surprises over the years. All over the sub-continent producing amazing cakes is a real art. Tashi had a marvellous third birthday cake baked in Kathmandu; it was a vision in mustard yellow, candy pink and lime green with icing flowers, three candles and 'Happy Birthday' in English and Nepali.

Eating in restaurants is a mixed pleasure with children. Usually children enjoy eating out, but it does require a fairly sensible attitude. Choose restaurants that are not too crowded, possibly by eating earlier you can miss the crowds. Restaurants where you can eat outside are also worth looking out for. Check the menu to make sure there is something your children can eat. If there isn't a high chair and you have to have a child on your knee, don't order soup.

Servings

Older children make for easier dining companions, but in general the amount of food served in restaurants is too much for a small child. While a sandwich may sound the right size it can come with chips (French fries) and salad which remain untouched. Entrees (appetisers) are often the right amount of food for children, or sharing a meal between two can work out if both people can agree on what to share! Tony and I often order three dishes for four of us and then everyone takes what they want (in some restaurants two meals are adequate).

Treats

Compromise is a necessary attribute for travelling families, but really it is the parents who have to compromise. Your children would be perfectly happy to stay home; this trip is your idea. If you want them to have a positive attitude towards travel you must meet them halfway. You can always go without a meal but your children can't. If your children are feeling a little bit homesick, familiar food can help to allay the feeling that home has disappeared. A splurge on a milkshake or ice cream can often work wonders and is well worth the money spent.

I remember one particularly miserable trip in Java, Indonesia. There were endless hours in a crowded, slow and very uncomfortable bemo. We finally arrived at a rather gloomy hotel in Bandung just as it began to pour with rain. We were all tired, fed up and rather cranky. Tony went out and scouted around while I tried to cheer up the children; after a little while he was back with the news that we were close to a great place to eat and several cake shops. Off we went: a good spaghetti bolognese, pizza, soft drink, followed by a visit to the cake shops, then back to the hotel carrying three little boxes of disgusting looking cakes, to find that there was a video showing *Teenwolf* with Michael J Fox. It all had absolutely nothing to do with why you go to Java, but the day had been completely turned around and the kids thought Bandung was terrific!

Alternatives

There are occasions when a restaurant is not a good idea: when you have been out all afternoon, and now it's dinner time and the baby is tired, and you all feel a bit strained and hungry. An older child may express their misery with a continuous, aggravating whine. This is not the time to be shushing them and pointing out that the whole restaurant is watching, that will only raise the decibel level. At times like this a quiet meal in your room can be a terrific alternative.

Room Service Room service is one way of doing it. The inflated prices and sometimes mediocre food which seem to come with room service are nothing compared to the joy of not having to set out to find a restaurant, find something everyone can eat, keep the children awake and happy through the process of ordering and waiting for food to arrive and then persuade them to eat something.

Children usually really enjoy room service (little hedonists) and if it is kept for those special occasions, the idea of a 'treat' may cheer them up completely. In the privacy of your room they can eat how they like, in their pyjamas perhaps, ready to go to bed right after. There will be a mess of course, so try to avoid eating on the beds.

Takeaways Even cheap hotels can usually send someone out to get takeaways for you. In Asia there always seems to be a local restaurant or cafe just around the corner where the hotel staff send out for noodles or tea, eating out is quite a corner-stone of Asian life and takeaways probably were invented here!

Alternatively one of the parents can go on a food-gathering mission to a local

TRAVEL TIPS...

Always carry a mop-up cloth, bibs, wet wipes and other cleaning apparatus.

fast food place, a restaurant with takeaways, or even to a night market or food stall. Some places in Asia are quite ingenious at devising take-away packages, as are restaurants and coffee shops.

Utensils & Equipment

Carry spout cups for small children to have their drinks from; this can save a lot of spills. If they refuse to be seen drinking from spout cups, teach them to drink through straws which they can usually manage from an early age. Always carry a mop-up cloth, bibs, wet wipes and other cleaning apparatus. It helps to have your own plate and spoon, so that you can organise a small portion for your child without having to wait for the waiter to bring you what you need, or go through the sometimes frustrating task of trying to get him to understand that you really want an extra empty plate.

FOOD
Breastfeeding

Babies are easy. If you are travelling with a baby under 12-months-old it is much easier to breastfeed. I have read in some book on travelling with children that nursing mothers may lose or diminish their milk supply while travelling. I suppose the idea is that it is tiring and anxiety provoking. Well it may be, but I don't know of any mother yet who has had this happen to her.

I can't think of anything more tiring or anxiety-causing than the alternative: trying to feed a child with a bottle and formula while travelling. How would you keep the bottle sterile? How would you get it to the right temperature while travelling on a bus in Java? How do you make up the formula with the necessary clean water? What happens when your baby wants a drink on the road, or in a hotel bedroom at 3 am? How do you keep the formula good in a humid climate without a fridge? The mind boggles.

One way you can ensure your milk supply does not diminish is to breast-feed whenever the baby wants to drink. This will probably be very frequently. I found that the best way of dealing with night feeds was to take the baby into bed with me and just let them get on with it; I was vaguely aware during the night when they fed, but I didn't need to become totally conscious and it wasn't nearly so tiring.

Don't try to race around and see everything in a hurry. Go easy on yourself, slow down, then you will be less tired and more relaxed. Drink lots of fluid and make sure you eat properly. All the usual advice to nursing mothers applies when you are travelling.

Since most mothers are not likely to be taking newborn babies travelling (three-months-old is probably early enough), you shouldn't have to worry about what you eat. I love curries and ate what I felt like, and it didn't seem to bother either Tashi or Kieran, although they may have become acclimatised in the womb!

Nor will it affect the child if you have a stomach upset, although you must be extremely careful not to pass the bug on to the baby due to lack of hygiene. Make sure you wash your hands thoroughly, and frequently.

Bottlefeeding

If you are bottlefeeding your baby the main issues will be: clean water and sterile equipment. Formula must be made up with either bottled, purified or boiled water.

Made-up formula deteriorates quickly so bottles should be made up as the baby needs them or refrigerated and used within 24 hours. The bottles and teats you use to feed the baby must be sterilised by either boiling them for ten minutes or using Milton or some other sterilising tablets.

Most Asian countries will have tins of baby formula available in familiar Western brands. The widespread practice of feeding babies formula has been a controversial issue for some years; critics claim that Western companies are pushing their products on developing countries as a viable alternative to breastfeeding, failing to admit that it is never as good as the real thing. In developing countries there is also the very real danger that the formula may be mixed with contaminated water.

If you are travelling in developing

TRAVEL TIPS...

...an empty, cylindrical baby-wipe container... was just big enough to make an ideal sterilising unit – fill with water, add the tab and bottle and teat, put the lid on and leave overnight.

countries you should be very careful before using formula as it may not have been stored in ideal conditions. Check the expiry date, ensure the packaging has not been opened, and where it has to be mixed with water be absolutely sure that the water is safe.

Sterilising Bottles If your child drinks from a bottle carry two small plastic bottles and teats and some sterilising tablets. Each night you can ask your hotel or restaurant for some boiled water to sterilise the bottles. I found that an empty, cylindrical baby-wipe container, thoroughly cleaned, was just big enough to make an ideal sterilising unit – fill with water, add the tab and bottle and teat, put the lid on and leave overnight.

Food Rules

The food in developing countries is often very good – it certainly won't be shot full of chemicals and preservatives the way so much of ours is. But in many places hygiene leaves a lot to be desired and you have to be careful about what your children eat. What won't affect your stomach may well prove disastrous to your children's less-hardened digestive system.

The basic rules apply when eating out in developing countries. While you have to be very careful where your children eat, and endeavour to ensure that everything is hygienically prepared and served, don't become too paranoid. You will soon get a feel for where to eat. Restaurants that are popular and crowded are usually OK; no restaurant lasts for long if it's poisoning its patrons! Restaurants that are crowded with Western travellers will also usually be producing food that appeals to Western tastes. There seems to be a travellers' menu that has spread throughout the world with familiar features like fruit salad, pancakes, French fries, yoghurt and so on.

Solid Food

When your baby requires a few extras in the food line you can generally find plenty to suit. Mashed bananas can be prepared almost anywhere and scrambled eggs are just about always available. A lot of Chinese food is suitable for children; steamed chicken, noodles, sweet corn and chicken soup. I found that Tashi at six-months-old just loved

BASIC FOOD RULES

Choose only the cleanest-looking restaurants.

Don't feed your child raw salads, or uncooked food. It is best to buy fruit from the market, wash it in purified water and peel it yourself.

Don't add water to juice or wash your babies' utensils with water unless you know it has been boiled. Always keep bottled or boiled and purified water. For boiled water to be absolutely safe, it has to have been boiled for at least 10 minutes, so if you are in doubt add purifying tabs as an extra precaution.

Wash your own and your child's hands before you eat. Many restaurants will have hand basins with soap and towels. Asians in particular are usually very careful about this aspect of hygiene, although the towels supplied may look rather grotty. If you carry your wet wipes you can clean up whenever necessary.

Chinese food and managed to find out for herself what she liked. She used to just help herself from my plate, but became a little more cautious after trying a mouthful of curry.

Don't be too dogmatic about what your children can and can't eat, although obviously the normal rules still apply to avoiding choking your child on bones and the like. Indian children are introduced to spices from an early age; although you shouldn't start sprinkling chilli on your baby's scrambled egg, if you let them help themselves whenever they show interest you will soon find out what they will and won't eat.

I have never used the commercially-prepared baby foods at home, but I did carry a few jars as a back-up when we travelled and once or twice they were useful. There are also dried food preparations which have to be mixed with hot water or milk. Cereals are often a very useful stand-by to have with you. These are easy to pack and keep, but you will have to be careful to use properly boiled/sterilised water or milk when making them up too. You can often buy these in the kind of stores that will have disposable nappies.

Dairy Products

Milk and other dairy products are not eaten widely in many societies outside the Western world. Cheese is available in tins in some countries and you often come across it in places frequented by Western travellers. Prepackaged, flavoured yoghurt is available in many countries and plain yoghurt is a familiar locally-made food in places all over the world. Yoghurt is available all over the Indian subcontinent and it can be really delicious. It is known as curd and is made from goat's or buffalo's milk.

Familiar Food

It is a good idea to give in to demands for familiar food from time to time. If you try to stick too rigidly to an eating budget, or insist that you eat local food 'because you can always get a sandwich at home' or 'when in Thailand eat what the Thais eat' you will find yourself with a rebellious child whose determination is usually greater than yours.

There have been occasions when despite the different language the children have instantly recognised the local equivalent of 'Burger King' or 'Kentucky Fried Chicken'. Tony and I retain our ideological purity by letting the children eat there, then they have to come and watch us eat at a place of our choice, and afterwards we find common ground on dessert!

Self-Catering

Sometimes you can prepare a meal yourself. Noodles are a great stand-by and most children will eat these. If you have an electric element for boiling water you could always use it to boil some two-minute noodles, which are available everywhere. Add a few pieces of fruit for dessert and another crisis has been averted with a minimum of fuss!

We have never carried a camping stove but I have had letters from travelling parents who feel that life on the road would have been impossible without one. There are various types on the market, but those that use kerosene or spirit would be more useful than Camping Gaz as you will be able to refill them just about anywhere, and you can empty them out to take on planes, whereas Camping Gaz cylinders may not be widely available and you cannot carry them on planes.

The packets and/or jars of baby food that you have been toting around can prove very useful. Do anything that will fill your children's stomach without subjecting you all to unnecessary stress. It may put paid to your plans for the evening – you may have been dreaming all day of the dinner you would have at a favourite restaurant, you may be very hungry and want a 'real' meal, you may wish you had listened to your friends advice and stayed home – but remember that flexibility is a real attribute for any traveller and an absolute essential for a travelling parent.

Snacks

Always carry snacks with you, particularly if you are going walking or travelling by bus, train or car. Even if you know there are shops around or the trip is scheduled for just an hour – remember that delays are not unusual and that when you arrive shops may not have anything suitable for your child to eat. So carry sultanas or raisins, nuts, an apple or orange (bananas go mushy very quickly), some juice or milk cartons, some bread or biscuits. Water is a necessity, for drinking and cleaning. Carry a knife for peeling and cutting fruit and a few jars of baby food just in case.

Biscuits are available just about everywhere and can be a special treat if your child is particularly tired and cranky and needs a bribe to go on. Marie biscuits, that venerable English standby, seem to have been left behind in every remote corner of the old British Empire. Children usually like them and you can get them in South-East Asia, on the Indian subcontinent and in Africa. The British Cadbury's brand of chocolates are also found worldwide.

Loss of Appetite

Try not to worry about how much your children are eating. There may be days when you think they are living on air, but they probably do that at home as well. Children eat when they are hungry, so don't start worrying that this trip will end with starved, malnourished children. Make an effort to find things that they can eat, and should like, but you can't do any more than that. Carry some children's multi-vitamin drops or tablets, make sure they drink a lot of water and milk, offer them plenty of fruit and after that relax.

DRINK

In parts of the world where the water is not safe to drink unless it has been boiled or properly purified, the usual advice to adults is to drink tea or coffee or commercial brands of bottled drinks. None of this advice is much use to small children. Possibly the only tea that is suitable for children and frequently available is chamomile, which has the added advantage of calming them and promoting sleep. However, generally babies are not very enthusiastic about tea or coffee and you have long years ahead trying to persuade them not to drink too many Cokes, so you don't want to start them on a soft drink habit at six months of age.

Water
Fortunately in recent years bottled mineral water (so called) has become widely available in many countries, especially in Asia. While the one-litre plastic bottles are the cause of major litter problems in some places, you can at least get safe drinking water fairly readily. You should always have a water bottle with bottled, boiled or purified water with you.

Juice
Also handy are the small individual cartons of fruit drinks, complete with sealed straw, which are now familiar almost throughout the world. They make a great safe alternative to soft drinks and are easily transportable so if you're travelling in a remote region it's a good idea to stock up on them when you find them.

You can also make fruit juice yourself by squeezing oranges, either by hand or with a plastic squeezer/juicer. In many places fresh fruit juices are available from stalls where you can see them being made, so you can make sure they don't add ice or water unless you're sure it's been purified.

Soft Drinks
When they're a bit older the soft drinks alternative does come in. You may not be happy having your children drink too many of them but reputable major brands of soft drinks are produced under hygienic conditions and are quite safe. It is, however, easy to fall into the soft drinks trap, where you end up buying soft drinks several times a day because it is hot and at least the drinks are safe. We try to stick to a one-soft-drink-a-day rule; the rest of the time it is juice or our own treated water, possibly flavoured with powder. The children accept this and look forward to their 'treat' and we find that they will often decide for themselves they don't really want a soft drink, especially where there are good fresh juices. Forbidding soft drinks completely is difficult when you are exposed to them so often (eating in restaurants, etc) and gives the children something else to complain about when they feel grumpy.

Milk & Soy Milk
Milk is not as widely available or drunk as much in developing countries as it is in the West, although even in India it is often possible to find. Where it is not pre-packaged it is usually just boiled and served hot, or with a chunk of ice to cool it down. I have drunk it often, especially when I was pregnant and needing extra calcium, but only freshly boiled milk is safe to drink and avoid the ice.

Cows are not always well cared for in developing countries and the hygiene surrounding the milking process may be inadequate. The storage and transportation of the milk may also be suspect. Finally, keep in mind that tuberculosis can be contracted by drinking unpasteurised milk.

These days in South-East Asia and

increasingly in other parts of the world you will find cartons of long-life milk, plain or flavoured. This is excellent and can be a real life saver with young children. Soy bean milk is also available in cartons in South-East Asia, but most brands have sugar added.

BABYSITTERS

Babysitters are a possibility in many countries. Large hotels in tourist areas can often make babysitting arrangements, but it's much nicer when the little local hotel in which you are staying is run by a family, and the daughters would just love to look after your children. You can come to some arrangement as to when and how much; usually it will be a very small financial cost. If you are planning a long stay in one place, you can often organise someone to look after the children. Enquire at your hotel, or if you know someone in the area ask them to check it out for you.

In general even young children (by our standards) will be very competent baby minders. Most young girls have been trained by looking after their younger siblings. Children as young as five often have total responsibility for little babies while their parents work.

While I don't suggest you hire a five-year-old, children from 11 years upwards will usually be a competent 'nanny'. In Asia in particular I really don't feel you have to be as cautious or wary with strangers as you would in most Western countries. Obviously there is always some uneasiness with people you don't know, but certainly in the villages and smaller places your children should be perfectly safe with a local child minder. Leave snacks and drinks, make sure they understand that your children are not to drink the local water. For the first few times you leave them, try to be gone for only a short time and tell the babysitter when you will be back. If you have any instructions make sure they are understood – get an interpreter if necessary.

With very small children it doesn't really matter whether the babysitter speaks English – 'no' is fairly clear in most languages – but with older children it will help if the babysitter speaks even a little English. Tashi and Kieran have enjoyed a wide variety of babysitters and were quite happy to sit and draw with those who didn't speak English very well or at all. The three of them used pictures to communicate, drawing houses, animals and so on and giving the names of things they drew in both languages. I found the babysitters enjoyed this as much as the children.

Nowadays the children disdain babysitters and are often quite happy to stay in the hotel room and watch TV. (Star TV, in Asia, provides reruns of ancient *Neighbours* episodes and up-to-the-minute basketball games direct from the USA.)

USA

Michael & Bennie Lyon discovered California at the ages of seven and five. Their parents, James & Pauline, were much older.

KIDS LOVE SOUTHERN CALIFORNIA, but is California really kiddie friendly, or does it only love kids for their parents' money? So long as the parents can afford it, So-Cal can provide it. Even our jaded kids found daily diversions which they judged to be so cool (the ultimate accolade) that we smiled indulgently and didn't dwell on the credit limit looming over our various pieces of plastic. The great glory of California is that it can make the most miserly shoestring travellers feel good about blowing their budget.

On a practical level, it's one of the easiest, safest and most convenient places to travel with kids. For example, just about any restaurant will have a high chair, and a children's menu, and a paper placemat with puzzles and pencils to keep them amused while they wait for their meal. You don't have to ask – the kiddie equipment just appears. And the food is served promptly, generally within the attention span of a five-year-old. And if they don't eat it all, you can always get a 'to go' box for the leftovers.

Of course, a lot of California's child care and child entertainment is highly commercialised, as we found at Sea World in San Diego. It's a superb complex with brilliant displays of marine life, but at $28 for adults and $20 for kids it ain't cheap – and the cost of food, drinks and souvenirs can easily add another $50. The dolphin petting pool was too crowded at first, so we raced around to the walrus show, the shark encounter and the otter exhibit. We visited the 'Forbidden Reef', saw Shamu the killer whale, scoffed $2 bags of popcorn and resisted the pressure to buy stuffed effigies of the star performers. But Michael was yearning to pat a dolphin, so we made it back there before closing time. With his arms plunged in the chilly water, he whistled, called and begged with heart-rending sincerity. But the closest he came was a fleeting touch of the hard, smooth, almost slimy bodies as they sped past in search of someone with the sardines that are sold as dolphin food – for about a dollar a half dozen. At that stage the sardine stall had closed for the day, and my enduring memory of Sea World is of my seven-year-old son leaning over the pool in tears of disappointment as the dolphins cruised by disdainfully beneath a gorgeous golden sunset. And those hard-nosed dolphins summed up something about southern California – huge smiles and beautiful bodies, but if you don't have negotiable currency they'll always be just out of reach.

In many public places kids are often regarded as either a nuisance or a potential legal liability. Our boys played in fountains and climbed balconies all over Mexico, but they couldn't get away with that in a Mexican restaurant just 10 miles north of the border. 'I'm sorry, but you'll have to stop the kids playing in the fountain – they might splash water on the ground.' 'I'm sorry, our insurance doesn't cover us for kids running on the patio.' 'Please stop your kids going onto the balcony – they might get their heads stuck in the railing, fall over the edge, slip down the stairs, hurt themselves, and make a mess in the foyer.' Much of this is litigation paranoia rather than real concern, but it can sure cramp a kid's style – and maybe there *are* some parents out there who only had kids so they could train them to be accident-prone and make millions sueing public liability insurers.

On a personal rather than a commercial level, it does seem that many Californians just don't like kids. Travellers talk as if the worst air disaster is being seated in the same row as a lap-child (that's what the airlines call passengers aged under two who pay 10% of the adult fare to not occupy a seat). Yuppie types expressed sympathy for us as parents, as if to say

'Don't you know how to prevent that sort of thing? It must seriously limit your lifestyle options.' And then they would roller-blade off to their self-actualisation workshop. Of course those Californians who do have kids care for them as much as parents anywhere, and if you're planning to travel to California with children it's worth making an effort to make contact with a local family. Then you can get beyond the commercial hype, and find the people wonderfully hospitable, and keen to show you the best the state has to offer.

It's a manifestation of the highly specialised economy that there are special places for children to do special children's things under the care of specially trained staff. With a TV in every hotel room and a fast-food franchise on every corner, our kids quickly learned their place in the market. To them, going somewhere different was going to Burger King instead of McDonald's, and trying something new became anything other than a Happy Meal. More than anywhere else, the free enterprise system gives kids what they *want*, even if it's not what their parents would like. Outside the kids' market sector, kids might be a nuisance, but within that sector they are the consumers, the kings; and the market meets their desires brilliantly.

> **'** *When I learned to ski it started with serious stuff about snow-ploughs and wedges, but in California they start by making their skis like a slice of pizza.* **'**

And no-one can top California's kid-care professionals for entertainment value and sheer enthusiasm. Take Bennie's ski class at Mammoth Mountain. After a two-second wait, the ski instructor appeared from stage left, skimming across the snow on nylon covered knees, and skidded to a halt in front of my five-year-old. 'Hey dude,' he said, 'Kevin's the name and skiing's the game. Gimme five!' Kevin was as good looking as a movie star, with an infectious grin and eyes that sparkled through the Ray-Bans. He and Bennie exchanged heavy-gloved high fives. 'Hey Ben,' he said, 'I bet you just love pizza.' When I learned to ski it started with serious stuff about snow-ploughs and wedges, but in California they start by making their skis like a slice of pizza. Bennie could relate to that. After three days of high spirited tuition with Kevin and his cohorts (at $38 a day), Bennie had not only mastered the pizza but was even starting to ski parallel, or, as they say in So-Cal, doing French fries. So long, and have a great day!

James Lyon

EUROPE

Julie Young (pictured with Sydney) lived and travelled in Europe when her son Sydney was a baby, before returning to Australia to live.

S YDNEY WAS BORN IN BERLIN, got his first tooth in Austria, learned to crawl in a campervan in the south of France and took his first steps in a long-since-deserted village in Spain. Without intention he had spent the first few years of his life marking Europe with his own triumphs of development.

In those years I undertook some mammoth journeys with him, none of which were more daunting than the prospect of carrying a bucketful of briquettes up five flights of stairs, babe in arms, in a wintry Berlin. Unlike most nesting mothers, my instinct was to roam, so as soon as Sydney was old enough, we left the last dregs of winter behind.

We travelled through most of Europe in a campervan with the essentials, sticking more or less to the usual bed/bath/sleeping/eating/playing time routine. A campervan gives you the freedom of being able to stop at any time; you still have the familiar four walls and bedding, and you can also cook your own food along the way. As Sydney grew older and needed more space, I became an expert at spotting playgrounds, which were not only a good source of socialising for him, but also enabled me to watch how other cultures interact with their children. I learned a lot from those playground days; if ever anyone showed the slightest interest in my child and could utter a few good English words, I would quickly whip out my pen and paper and get them to jot down names, in their language, of anything I may need at the chemist, doctor or the supermarket. I also learned a great deal about European food and the best wines of the region. In multi-cultural Melbourne, I still love the parks and playgrounds, though you have to find the right ones.

Another winter Sydney and I embarked upon a 30-hour train ride from Berlin to Barcelona to visit some friends. On a German train, quite soon into the journey, I realised that my child's curiosity and behaviour was frowned upon, and I was told that I should look for the compartment marked 'women and children' in the next carriage. What a great relief it was to walk into a train compartment of animated kids running amok, in a space that belonged to them. Germany, I discovered, has a very supportive and practical attitude to children, providing they are not around, and I made a note to look and ask in future.

> ❛ *...a rather lively discussion was in progress about the fact that Sydney would soon wake up and need some milk...the conductor would leap out of the moving train, run back 500 metres to the last station and dive back on board with a baby's bottle full of perfectly warmed milk.* ❜

On the next leg of the journey we had to change trains at some ungodly hour and boarded a commuter train to take us from the border to Barcelona. There everyone noticed my sleeping child but, rather than having to move, I could tell that he was welcome. The woman sitting beside me pointed to him, and to the empty baby's bottle in my hand. When I did not understand, she invited the whole carriage to join in the conversation. Unbeknown to me, a rather lively discussion was in progress about the fact that Sydney would soon wake up and need some milk, and if everyone was agreeable, the conductor would leap out of the moving train, run back 500 metres to the last station and dive back on board with a baby's bottle full of perfectly warmed milk. Oh how I loved Spain.

Once we had arrived in the old and derelict village where friends lived with their children, I moaned to discover that 'old and 'derelict' meant no electricity or running water. However I enjoyed learning to adapt with makeshift and basic equipment, and all the kids seemed happy and unaware of the lack of modern conveniences. The kids delighted in the trips to the spring to collect water, and the highlight of their week was when the shepherd came and ran his flock through the village.

We left Europe and returned via Perth, to Melbourne, where we settled into a regular routine. On our first break we headed north to Byron Bay and stayed in a backpacker hostel, at the same time humpback whales were in the area. I decided on a backpack rather than a stroller, thinking that at the age of four, Syd would walk everywhere and the stroller would just be a cumbersome nuisance.

In retrospect, a stroller would have been very useful, especially at times when we were waiting for buses and planes which were delayed. It would have also been useful for transporting luggage and thus being able to keep pace with a flighty child. As left-luggage facilities seem to be non-existent around Coolangatta, carrying a large backpack and a sleeping four-year-old was a painful experience.

However, my choice of backpacker accommodation was a smart decision, and suited us both. We took a private room and shared the kitchen, bathroom and lounge room and this arrangement gave Sydney a sense of belonging to a community and made him feel comfortable and secure.

On our third evening there I promised Syd a BBQ, and cooking my four pitiful sausages, I was surprised to see a group of hungry and expectant people join us. Realising some confusion, they announced: 'We're here for the BBQ, Sydney invited us'. For a sole parent holding down a full-time job, turning bread into sausages was no great feat.

Julie Young

FIJI

Kate Cody (pictured with Jackson) & Ben Taylor travelled to Fiji when Jackson was 6 months old.

BEN AND I TRAVELLED TO FIJI WHEN JACKSON WAS 6-MONTHS-OLD, fully breastfed and only just starting on solids. He could sit but not crawl and he hadn't started teething so we figured we should travel while the odds were still in our favour.

We had booked a room at the *Royal Hotel* in Levuka (the old capital of Fiji) for our holiday because it sounded ramshackle, chaotic and atmospheric. We also had friends who had stayed there a year before who said it was like the Pacific version of Fawlty Towers. The incongruity of the image was tantalising and the five-hour flight seemed an easy way to test our ability to travel with a baby.

While there was no Basil or Sybil at the Royal, the services provided were minimal and the people who ran the place could never be accused of selling out. The Ashley family hadn't made any concessions in the face of increasing tourism, competition from upmarket resorts on the main island, and the expectations of '90s travellers.

I had booked in advance and they had organised a cot and a small fridge for our room. So we had the basics. We used to go out early to eat dinner, then return to the room to put Jackson to bed. Once he was tucked away we would try to read in the light that spilled in from the bathroom, too scared to turn on the overhead lamp in case he woke.

Jackson woke as often as four times a night just to check that the breast was still on offer. And while I always wished that I could get even half an hour more sleep I was glad that I could calm him easily in the dead of night. More to the point, I didn't think that it was feasible to embark on a programme of control crying: the walls were so thin that I could hear every cough and spit from the man in the next room.

One day we trekked over a steep, slippery mountain to the village at the centre of the island. Ben carried Jackson on his back the whole way and I concentrated on looking for wild papaya for our guide who wanted to take some back to his home village. Jackson, who should have been lulled to sleep by the movement, screamed most of the way and would not be soothed with milk. I felt increasingly stressed by the crying until our guide took Jackson on his back and eventually managed to make him laugh by skipping along the path.

> **'The school children walked along with us holding on to Jackson's dangling feet and sticky fists. '**

After four hours we reached the village and walked between the rows of timber houses. Our guide called his greetings through open doorways to the families within and explained who we were. We climbed the grassy hill above the village to the white weatherboard school and all the children came running out to see us. They hadn't seen a fat white baby in their village before! The school children walked along with us holding on to Jackson's dangling feet and sticky fists. Driving back to town by bus along the shoreline, nursing a sleeping baby, the feeling of contentment outweighed the awareness of the effort it took to get there.

The refreshing thing about travelling with a baby is that people go out of their way to help you and include you. We benefited from many small acts of kindness while we were in Levuka, purely because as a family we were in a different category: no longer the alien traveller.

As we had only a shower in our room Mrs Ashley gave us a large red plastic tub to put in the bottom of the recess to bathe Jackson in. And while they discouraged us from eating at the hotel because they didn't want to prepare food for us, each morning the cook would bring an out-of-season mango to our room for Jackson to taste. I bought sweet potato, taro, apple and pear at the local market and the staff at the hotel willingly cooked them for the baby.

The last day we were in Levuka was Saturday and the home team was playing soccer against Suva. The oval was just behind our hotel so we watched the whole town turn out on foot or in trucks, unpacking children, dogs, umbrellas, food and beer. We decided to go too and picked our way through the crowd. As the only white family we really stood out. All afternoon women with babies of their own would approach me to ask questions about Jackson: boy or girl? how old? how many kilos? They would smell his skin, kiss him and cuddle him and compare him to their own babies. Even though Levuka was their town and I came from somewhere else, I was welcomed because I was a mother like them.

Katie Cody

BALI

Bennie Lyon (pictured with Balinese woman) had his 2nd birthday in Bali when his brother Michael was three years old. They have returned twice with their parents, James and Pauline.

THE FIRST TIME WE WENT AWAY WITH OUR KIDS, Bennie was still in nappies. As much as anything else, we did it to prove we still could – we weren't going to admit that parenthood would make us give up travelling. Besides, everyone said that the Balinese just *love* children.

Actually, the nappies were one of the first dilemmas. Do we take disposables, even if they're not environmentally friendly, or cloth nappies, in which case how do we wash them? Our guidebook said that Balinese babies used neither, and to be careful when they sit on your knee. It also pointed out that disposable nappies, though bulky, are light, so one can carry dozens of the things in a duffel bag, then stuff the bag with sarongs, T-shirts, woodcarvings and whatever on the way back. These days, disposable nappies are freely available on Bali, and sometimes make up a distasteful component in local litter. Even when properly disposed of, they contribute to the solid-waste problem on what is, after all, a small and very densely populated island.

Using cloth nappies on Bali was not much more hassle than using them at home – rinse them in the bath with the hand-held shower head, soak them in a plastic bucket, hand wash them in the handbasin, and hang them on the verandah to dry. The typical Balinese *losmen* (family-run inn) is well set up for this. The bathrooms are designed to have water splashed around them, as in the traditional *mandi* (wash) which involves throwing water all over oneself with a coconut shell. The hot weather makes the nappy chore refreshing, and they dry soon enough despite the humidity. Plastic water buckets have largely replaced coconut shells in the *mandi* and elsewhere, and are available for the asking at even the most basic losmen – the Balinese have a way of making even a plastic bucket seem like a traditional artefact, almost a natural object.

> **' There is a belief that babies come straight from God, and the younger they are, the closer they are to the divine powers. '**

It is true that the Balinese love children, especially young children, and they are a real social asset to travel with. There is a belief that babies come straight from God, and the younger they are, the closer they are to the divine powers. Even at increasingly ungodly ages, you will find your kids the subject of much admiration and curiosity. Once I saw an old lady pinching the front of Bennie's nappy to ascertain whether he was a boy or a girl. After grasping the truth, and noting that Michael was also male, she seemed delighted at how lucky we were; 'larky' she exclaimed, 'larky larky'. I figured that male children were highly valued in Bali. Later that I found out that *laki* means boy in Indonesian; *laki laki* is the plural. And a *perempuan* (girl) is equally valued. Travelling with children opens up great new possibilities for cross-cultural misunderstanding.

Children in Bali are the responsibility of their whole community, not just a problem for their parents alone. So when one of our kids toddled towards the door of a restaurant, heading for the busy street outside, someone would always scoop him up, cuddle him, and maybe play with him for a while before reluctantly returning him to us. At home in Australia, the more common reaction would be to point out to the parents that their kid was on the loose and they should do something about it. An unfortunate consequence of the Balinese attitude is the absence of many safety facilities which Western families regard as basic. Steep stairways, unfenced drops and unguarded swimming pools are common, while car seatbelts and bicycle helmets are rarely encountered. Because children are regarded as a normal part of the community, they share the same furniture, food and transport as everyone else – few restaurants have children's menus or high chairs, babysitting services are rarely advertised (though widely available if you ask), and kids are crammed into the *bemos* (local minibuses) along with the adults, vegetables and livestock.

Another consequence of the communal nature of Balinese life is that parenting practices are the subject of public scrutiny. Balinese get most upset if a young child is allowed to cry, and will often pick it up, find the mother, and hand the noisy one over with a reproachful look and a suggestion that it be fed

travel stories

immediately. *Tidak boleh* (no crying) is a maxim of Balinese child rearing. Sometimes they despair altogether of uncaring Western parents, and the child will be whisked off to a place where it can be cuddled, cosseted and fed. The initial approach to quieting a crying infant is usually to insert a ripe banana into the screaming orifice – it often works. On one occasion, after Bennie had been thus silenced, I asked the young paediatric expert why one rarely heard Balinese babies cry. Her answer was succinct, but it didn't reveal whether the basis of this treatment was therapeutic or merely acoustic. 'Mouth full, not cry' she said.

> **' The initial approach to quieting a crying infant is usually to insert a ripe banana into the screaming orifice. '**

It only took us about a day to discover that smacking one's children is not socially acceptable on Bali. It took our sons only a fraction longer to realise that this was the case, that our usual threats were hollow, and that they could get away with things on Bali which would have painful consequences at home. I'm not talking about major child abuse here, but if the ultimate punishment in your family is a smack on the offending hand, you'd be wise to develop some alternative strategies before you arrive in Bali. Otherwise, put your darlings in the care of a Balinese *pembantu* (nanny) – they know more magic than Mary Poppins.

James Lyon

HEALTH

Travel health depends on your predeparture preparations, your day-to-day health care while travelling and how you handle any medical problem or emergency that does develop. While the list of potential dangers can seem quite frightening, with a little luck, some basic precautions and adequate information few travellers experience more than upset stomachs.

Our children have travelled with us in Africa, Australia, New Zealand, the Pacific, numerous places in Asia and in North and South America and never had any health problems.

Travel Health Guides

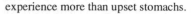

There are a number of books on travel health:

Staying Healthy in Asia, Africa & Latin America, Moon Publications. Probably the best all-round guide to carry, as it's compact but very detailed and well organised.
Travellers' Health, Dr Richard Dawood, Oxford University Press. Comprehensive, easy to read, authoritative and also highly recommended, although it's rather large to lug around.
Where There is No Doctor, David Werner, Hesperian Foundation. A very detailed guide intended for someone, like a Peace Corps worker, going to work in an undeveloped country, rather than for the average traveller.

Predeparture Preparations

Health Insurance A travel insurance policy to cover theft, loss and medical problems is a wise idea. There are a wide variety of policies and your travel agent will have recommendations. The international student travel policies handled by STA Travel or student travel organisations are usually good value. Some policies offer lower and higher medical expenses options but the higher one is chiefly for countries like the USA which have extremely high medical costs. Check the small print:

1. Some policies specifically exclude 'dangerous activities' which can include scuba diving, motorcycling, even trekking. If such activities are on your agenda you you will need another sort of policy.

A locally acquired motor cycle licence may not be valid under your policy.

2. You may prefer a policy which pays doctors or hospitals direct rather than you having to pay on the spot and claim later. If you have to claim later make sure you keep all documentation. Some policies ask you to call back (collect) to a centre in your home country where an immediate assessment of your problem is made.

3. Check if the policy covers ambulances or an emergency flight home. You may also need to cover the expanse of an additional person to accompany you in the case of certain

illnesses. If you have to stretch out you will need two seats and somebody has to pay for them!

Medical Kit A small, straightforward medical kit put together with special thought for children's ailments is a wise thing to carry.

Make sure that you know the appropriate children's dose of any medicines you are carrying, and that they are in fact suitable for children.

Ideally antibiotics should be administered only under medical supervision and should never be taken indiscriminately. Take only the recommended dose at the prescribed intervals and continue using the antibiotic for the prescribed period, even if the illness seems to be cured earlier. Antibiotics are quite specific to the infections they can treat. Stop immediately if there are any serious reactions and don't use the antibiotic at all if you are unsure that you have the correct one for the infection.

In many countries, if a medicine is available at all it will generally be available over the counter and the price will be much cheaper than in the West. However, be careful if buying drugs in developing countries, particularly where the expiry date may have passed or correct storage conditions may not have been followed. Bogus drugs are common and it's possible that drugs which are no longer recommended, or have even been banned, in the West are still being dispensed in many developing countries.

MEDICAL KIT

Infant analgesic – with measuring cup or dropper.

Antihistamine (such as Benadryl) – useful as a decongestant for colds, allergies, to ease the itch from insect bites or stings or to help prevent motion sickness. Antihistamines may have a sedative effect and interact with alcohol so care should be taken when using them.

Antibiotics – useful if you're travelling well off the beaten track, but it must be prescribed and you should carry the prescription with you. Some people are allergic to commonly prescribed antibiotics such as penicillin or sulfa drugs. Kaolin preparation (Pepto-Bismol), Imodium – for stomach upsets.

Rehydration mixture – for treatment of severe diarrhoea. This is particularly important if travelling with children who dehydrate easily. An electrolyte mixture is available in sachets.

Antiseptic (like Dettol or Betadine), mercurochrome and antibiotic powder or similar 'dry' spray – for cuts and grazes.

In many countries it may be a good idea to leave unwanted medicines, syringes etc with a local clinic, rather than carry them home.

Health Preparations Make sure you and your children are healthy before you start travelling. If you are embarking on a long trip make sure your teeth are OK; there are lots of places where a visit to the dentist would be the last thing you'd want to do.

If children wear glasses take a spare pair and the prescription. Losing glasses can be a real problem, although in many places you can get new spectacles made up quickly, cheaply and competently.

If your kids require a particular medication take an adequate supply, as it may not be available locally. Take the prescription or, better still, part of the packaging showing the generic rather than the brand name (which may not be locally available), as it will make getting replacements easier. It's a wise idea to have a legible prescription with you to show you legally use the medication – it's surprising how often over-the-counter drugs from one place are illegal without a prescription or even banned in another country.

Immunisations Vaccinations provide protection against diseases you might meet along the way. For some countries no immunisations are necessary, but the further off the beaten track you go the more necessary it is to take precautions.

Calamine lotion – to ease irritation from sunburn, bites or stings.

Bandages, band-aids, gauze and cotton wool – for minor injuries.

Scissors, tweezers and a thermometer/fever strips – mercury thermometers are prohibited by airlines.

Insect repellent, sun blocker, suntan lotion, chap stick – check that it is suitable for children's skin

Water purification tablets.

Nappy rash cream, teething gel – for predictable ailments.

Worm treatment, lice shampoo, anti-fungal powder – for treatment of minor but irritating health problems

A couple of syringes – in case you need injections in a country with medical hygiene problems. Ask your doctor for a note explaining why you are carrying them.

It is important to understand the distinction between vaccines recommended for travel in certain areas and those required by law. Essentially the number of vaccines subject to international health regulations has been dramatically reduced over the last 10 years. Currently yellow fever is the only vaccine subject to international health regulations. Vaccination as an entry requirement is usually only enforced when coming from an infected area.

Occasionally travellers face bureaucratic problems regarding the cholera vaccine, even though all countries have dropped it as a health requirement for travel. Visiting some countries it may be wise to have the vaccine despite its poor protection: such as when travelling across Africa.

On the other hand a number of vaccines are recommended for different areas of travel. These may not be required by law but are recommended for your own personal protection.

All vaccinations should be recorded on an International Health Certificate, which is available from your physician or government health department.

Plan ahead for getting your vaccinations: some of them require an initial shot followed by a booster, while some vaccinations should not be given together. It is recommended you seek medical advice at least six weeks prior to travel.

Most children from Western countries will have been immunised against various diseases during childhood but your doctor may still recommend booster shots against measles or polio, diseases still prevalent in many developing countries. Apart from these, special vaccinations for travelling are not normally given to children under 12 months of age. Talk to your doctor.

Regardless of how you feel about inoculations, if you plan to take your children travelling you are placing them at some risk. In some parts of the world the infant mortality rate is horrendous and diseases which are no longer a problem in the West, due to widespread vaccination programmes, are still very serious health risks.

The period of protection offered by vaccinations differs widely and some are contraindicated if you are pregnant or likely to become pregnant within three months of the vaccination.

In some countries immunisations are available from airport or government health centres. Travel agents or airline offices will tell you where.

The possible list of vaccinations includes:

Smallpox Smallpox has now been wiped out worldwide, so immunisation is no longer necessary.

Cholera Not required by law but occasionally travellers face bureaucratic problems on some border crossings. Protection is poor and it lasts only six months. It is contraindicated in pregnancy.

Tetanus & Diphtheria Boosters are necessary every 10 years and protection is highly recommended.

Typhoid Available either as an injection or oral capsules. Protection lasts from one to three years and is useful if you are travelling for long periods in rural, tropical areas. You may get some side effects such as pain at the injection site, fever, headache and a general feeling of being unwell. A new single-dose injectable vaccine, which appears to have few side effects, is now available but is more expensive. Side effects are unusual with the oral form but stomach cramps may be one of these.

Infectious Hepatitis The most common travel-acquired illness which can be prevented by vaccination. Protection can be provided in two ways – either with the antibody gammaglobulin or with a new vaccine called Havrix (currently unavailable in the United States). Havrix provides long-term immunity (possibly more than 10 years) after an initial course of two injections and a booster at one year. It may be more expensive than gammaglobulin but certainly has many advantages, including length of protection and ease of administration. It takes about three weeks to provide satisfactory protection – hence the need for careful planning prior to travel. Gammaglobulin is not a vaccination but a ready-made antibody which has proven very successful in reducing the chances of hepatitis infection. Because it may interfere with the development of immunity, it should not be given until at least 10 days after administration of the last vaccine needed; it should also be given as close as possible to departure because it is at its most effective in the first few weeks after administration and the effectiveness tapers off gradually between three and six months.

Yellow Fever Protection lasts 10 years and is recommended where the disease is endemic, chiefly in Africa and South America. You usually have to go to a special yellow fever vaccination centre. Vaccination is contraindicated during pregnancy but if you must travel to a high-risk area it is probably advisable. Check with your doctor.

Meningitis This vaccination is recommended for visitors to Nepal and for visitors to some areas of Africa and Brazil.

It is given as a single injection and gives immunity for up to three years duration.

Tuberculosis TB is widespread throughout the developing world. Most Westerners will have been vaccinated at some time during their school years. For children vaccination is not deemed necessary unless they will be spending prolonged periods (say up to a year) in an area of risk.

Basic Rules

Care in what you eat and drink is the most important health rule. Stomach upsets are the most likely travel health problem (between 30% and 50% of travellers in a two-week stay experience this) but the majority of these upsets will be relatively minor. Don't become paranoid; trying the local food is part of the experience of travel, after all.

Water, Juice & Dairy Products The

number one rule is *don't drink the water* and that includes ice. If you don't know for certain that the water is safe always assume the worst. Reputable brands of bottled water or soft drinks are generally fine, although in some places bottles refilled with tap water are not unknown. Only use water from containers with a serrated seal – not tops or corks. Take care with fruit juice, particularly if water may have been added. Milk should be treated with suspicion, as it is often unpasteurised. Boiled milk is fine if it is kept hygienically and yoghurt is always good. Tea or coffee should also be OK, since the water should have been boiled.

Water Purification The simplest way

of purifying water is to boil it thoroughly. Vigorously boiling for five minutes should be satisfactory; however, at high altitude water boils at a lower temperature, so germs are less likely to be killed.

Simple filtering will not remove all dangerous organisms, so if you cannot boil water it should be treated chemically. Chlorine tablets (Puritabs, Steritabs or other brand names) will kill many but not all pathogens, including giardia and amoebic cysts. Iodine is very effective in purifying water and is available in tablet form (such as Potable Aqua), but follow the directions carefully and remember that too much iodine can be harmful.

If you can't find tablets, tincture of iodine (2%) or iodine crystals can be used. Four drops of tincture of iodine per litre or quart of clear water is the recommended dosage. The treated water should be left to stand for 20 to 30 minutes before drinking. Iodine crystals can also be used to purify water but this is a more complicated process, as you have to first prepare a saturated iodine solution. Iodine loses its effectiveness if exposed to air or damp so keep it in a tightly sealed container. Flavoured powder will disguise the taste of treated water and is a good idea when travelling with children.

Food There is an old colonial adage which says: 'If you can cook it, boil it or peel it you can eat it...otherwise forget it'. Salads and fruit should be washed with purified water or peeled where possible. Ice cream is usually OK if it is a reputable brand name, but beware of buying it from street vendors in developing countries in case the ice cream has melted and

been refrozen. Thoroughly cooked food is safest but not if it has been left to cool or if it has been reheated. Shellfish such as mussels, oysters and clams should be avoided as well as undercooked meat, particularly in the form of mince. Steaming does not make shellfish safe for eating.

If a place looks clean and well run and if the vendor also looks clean and healthy, then the food is probably safe. In general, places that are packed with travellers or locals will be fine, while empty restaurants are questionable. Busy restaurants mean the food is being cooked and eaten quickly with little standing around and is probably not being reheated.

Nutrition If your food is poor or limited in availability, if you're travelling hard and fast and missing meals, or if your children simply lose their appetite, they can soon start to lose weight and place their health at risk.

Make sure you have a well-balanced diet. Eggs, tofu, beans, lentils (dhal in India) and nuts are all safe ways to get protein. Fruit you can peel (bananas, oranges or mandarins for example) is always safe and a good source of vitamins. Try to eat plenty of grains in the form of rice and bread. Remember that although food is generally safer if it is cooked well, overcooked food loses much of its nutritional value. If your diet isn't well balanced or if food intake is insufficient, it's a good idea to take vitamin and iron pills.

In hot climates make sure your children drink enough – don't rely on them

BASIC HEALTH RULES

Make sure your children's hands are clean before they eat. Carry wet wipes or a damp flannel in a plastic bag everywhere in case water is not available.

Clean teeth and wash toothbrushes with bottled or boiled/purified water.

Don't eat raw fruit or vegetables unless they have been thoroughly washed in safe water or you have peeled the fruit.

Avoid water and ice unless it is bottled or has been boiled and/or purified. Assume that all water or fresh food that has been washed in water is unsafe unless you positively know otherwise.

For small children try to regularly sterilise utensils they use. Soaking them in safe water with a sterilising tab will do. An empty 'baby wipe' container, a plastic ice cream container or a large Tupperware box will make a fine sterilising unit.

feeling thirsty to indicate when they should drink. If you are breastfeeding be prepared to feed much more frequently, or remember to give frequent additional drinks from a bottle. Always carry a water bottle with you on long trips. Not needing to urinate or very dark yellow urine is a danger sign.

Excessive sweating can lead to loss of salt and therefore muscle cramping. Salt tablets are not a good idea as a preventative, but in places where salt is not used much adding salt to food can help.

Everyday Health A normal body temperature is 98.6°F or 37°C; more than 2°C higher is a 'high' fever. A normal adult pulse rate is 60 to 80 per minute (children 80 to 100, babies 100 to 140). You should know how to take a temperature and a pulse rate. As a general rule the pulse increases about 20 beats per minute for each °C rise in fever.

Respiration (breathing) rate is also an indicator of illness. Count the number of breaths per minute: between 12 and 20 is normal for adults and older children (up to 30 for younger children, 40 for babies). People with a high fever or serious respiratory illness (like pneumonia) breathe more quickly than normal. More than 40 shallow breaths a minute usually means pneumonia.

In Western countries with safe water and excellent human waste disposal systems we often take good health for granted. In years gone by, when public health facilities were not as good as they are today, certain rules attached to eating and drinking were automatically observed, such as washing your hands before a meal. It is important for people travelling in areas of poor sanitation to be aware of this and adjust their own personal hygiene habits.

Clean your kids' teeth with purified water rather than straight from the tap. Avoid climatic extremes: keep them out of the sun when it's hot, dress them warmly when it's cold. Avoid potential diseases by making sure they are dressed sensibly. They can get worm infections through walking barefoot or dangerous coral cuts by walking over coral without shoes. Avoid insect bites by covering bare skin when insects are around, by screening windows or beds or by using insect repellents. Seek local advice: if you're told the water is unsafe due to jellyfish, crocodiles or bilharzia, don't go in. In situations where there is no information, discretion is the better part of valour.

Medical Problems & Treatment

Potential medical problems can be broken down into several areas. First there are the climatic and geographical considerations – problems caused by extremes of temperature, altitude or motion. Then there are diseases and illnesses caused by either poor environmental sanitation, insect bites or stings, and animal or human contact. Simple cuts, bites or scratches can also cause problems.

Self-diagnosis and treatment can be risky, so wherever possible seek qualified help. Although we do give treatment dosages in this section, they are for emergency use only. Medical advice should be sought where possible before administering any drugs.

An embassy or consulate can usually recommend a good place to go for such advice. So can five-star hotels, although they often recommend doctors with five-star prices. (This is when that medical insurance really comes in useful!) In some places standards of medical attention are so low that for some ailments the best advice is to get on a plane and go somewhere else.

Fever

Children often have high fevers for little apparent reason and recover from them remarkably quickly. Carry a digital thermometer and, if your children are very young, fever strips (those little strips which will tell you immediately if your child does have a fever). I find it easier to use these in the first instance as most small children are not too cooperative when having to sit still with a thermometer in their mouths for the required time. If the strip does indicate fever, use the thermometer to find out just how hot your child is. As you would normally do, try to get medical help if the temperature is abnormally high. Fevers in small children can be quite dangerous.

The general rule with treating fevers is to get the child cool as quickly as possible. Remove all their clothes, sponge the child down with tepid water, place close to a fan, and try to get them to drink something cool. If the temperature is high, place them in a cool bath. The child won't want to go, and may shiver because they are hot, but you must bring the temperature down. Administer paracetamol (eg Panadol). Treat fevers seriously, and always call in medical help if you are at all concerned.

Children often run temperatures without ill effect: my most frightening experience was Kieran running a high fever when we were in Africa. We were all sleeping in a rather small tent whilst a herd of elephants grazed outside. One male elephant was acting quite aggressively towards our camp. Since I found the sound of elephants grazing right by my head rather unsettling to say the least, I was not sleeping very well. In the middle of the night Kieran woke up, delirious and very feverish. Trying to calm him, get his fever down, keep him quiet, so as not to alarm the elephants, while remaining calm myself, was not easy. I was sure he had malaria, meningitis, sleeping sickness, etc. Next day, a rather tired but otherwise totally healthy Kieran awoke; I was a complete wreck.

Climatic & Geographical Considerations

Sunburn In the tropics, the desert or at high altitude you can get sunburnt surprisingly quickly, even through cloud. Use a sunscreen and take extra care to cover areas which don't normally see sun, such as your feet. A hat provides added protection, and you should also use zinc cream or some other barrier cream for your nose and lips.

Apart from sunburn, there is evidence that damage from overexposure to the sun can lead to skin cancer in later life. Small children burn easily so always use sunscreen , even if you are only taking

them for a five-minute walk around the corner to get lunch. Remember the sun is at its strongest around noon, but for most of the day in many countries it is strong enough to burn a baby very severely. Early morning and late afternoon are fine times to take the children to the beach; it is usually warm enough to really enjoy the water and the sand, but not hot enough to do any harm. Still, an umbrella may be a good idea to take to the beach to use as a sunshade, especially if you have a small baby who is not yet crawling or walking.

Cover your children with a complete sunscreen any time they are in the sun (water-resistant if they will be in the water). A T-shirt or light cotton caftan will also give protection and can be worn in the water. It is possible to burn through the T-shirt, especially when it is wet, so be careful. The danger of sunburn is greater at the beach than anywhere else as the sun reflects off the sand and water.

If your children do get burnt calamine lotion is a good standby, but there are other lotions (such as Bepanthin) you can get. Have a pair of sandals or beach shoes on hand as the sand can get hot enough to burn, badly, little, tender-skinned feet.

Try to get your children to wear a hat – both my children when they were very small promptly ripped hats off as soon as I put them on but it is worth persevering.

Prickly Heat Prickly heat is an itchy rash caused by excessive perspiration trapped under the skin. It usually strikes people who have just arrived in a hot climate and whose pores have not yet opened sufficiently to cope with greater sweating. Keeping cool but bathing often, using a mild talcum powder or even resorting to air-conditioning may help until your children acclimatise. If the rash is very bad check with a local pharmacy. If there is a history of hives or other allergic reactions in your family, ask your doctor's advice before you leave. Sometimes an antihistamine cream or medication is useful in severe cases.

Heat Exhaustion Dehydration or salt deficiency can cause heat exhaustion. Take time to acclimatise to high temperatures and make sure your kids get sufficient liquids. Salt deficiency is characterised by fatigue, lethargy, headaches, giddiness and muscle cramps and in this case salt tablets may help. Vomiting or diarrhoea can deplete their liquid and salt levels. Anhydrotic heat exhaustion, caused by an inability to sweat, is quite rare. Unlike the other forms of heat exhaustion it is likely to strike people who have been in a hot climate for some time, rather than newcomers.

Heat Stroke This serious, sometimes fatal, condition can occur if the body's heat-regulating mechanism breaks down and the body temperature rises to dangerous levels. Long, continuous periods of exposure to high temperatures can leave you vulnerable to heat stroke. Children are particularly susceptible to heatstroke and you should avoid excessive activity when you first arrive in a hot climate.

The symptoms are feeling unwell, not sweating very much or at all and a high body temperature (39°C to 41°C). Where sweating has ceased the skin becomes flushed and red. Severe, throbbing headaches and lack of coordination will also occur, and the sufferer may be confused or aggressive. Eventually the victim will become delirious or convulse. Hospitalisation is essential, but meanwhile get victims out of the sun, remove their clothing, cover them with a wet sheet or towel and then fan continually.

Fungal Infections Hot weather fungal infections are most likely to occur on the scalp, between the toes or fingers (athlete's foot), in the groin (jock itch or crotch rot) and on the body (ringworm). You get ringworm (a fungal infection) from infected animals or by walking on damp areas, like shower floors.

To prevent fungal infections wear loose, comfortable clothes made from natural fibres such as cotton, wash frequently and dry carefully. If you do get an infection, wash the infected area daily with a disinfectant or medicated soap and water, and rinse and dry well. Apply an antifungal powder like the widely available Tinaderm. Try to expose the infected area to air or sunlight as much as possible. Wash all towels and underwear in hot water and change them as often as possible.

Babies wearing nappies provide the perfect conditions for fungal infections such as thrush. In hot climates avoid using plastic pants and try to leave the nappy off as much as possible. If you are breastfeeding and your baby gets thrush be extremely careful to wash your hands thoroughly after nappy changes so that you don't transfer the infection to your breasts and the baby's mouth.

Cold Too much cold is just as dangerous as too much heat, particularly if it leads to hypothermia. If you are trekking at high altitudes or simply taking a long bus trip over mountains, particularly at night, be prepared. In some countries (eg, Tibet, Chile) you should always be prepared for cold, wet or windy conditions even if you're just out walking or hitching.

Hypothermia occurs when the body loses heat faster than it can produce it and the core temperature of the body falls. Children are particularly susceptible to extreme temperatures. It is surprisingly easy to progress from very cold to dangerously cold due to a combination of wind, wet clothing, fatigue and hunger, even if the air temperature is above freezing. It is best to dress in layers: silk, wool and some of the new artificial fibres are all good insulating materials. A hat is important, as a lot of heat is lost through the head. A strong, waterproof outer layer is essential, as keeping dry is vital. Carry basic supplies, including food containing simple sugars to generate heat quickly and lots of fluid to drink.

Symptoms of hypothermia are exhaustion, numb skin (particularly toes and fingers), shivering, slurred speech, irrational or violent behaviour, lethargy, stumbling, dizzy spells, muscle cramps and violent bursts of energy. Irrationality may take the form of sufferers claiming they are warm and trying to take off their clothes.

To treat hypothermia, first get the person out of the wind and/or rain, remove their clothing if it's wet and replace it with dry, warm clothing. Give them hot liquids – not alcohol – and some high-kilojoule, easily digestible food. Do not rub victims but place them near a fire or in a warm (not hot) bath. This should be enough for the early stages of hypothermia, but if it has gone further it may be necessary to place victims in warm sleeping bags and get in with them.

Children are more susceptible to changes of temperature and lose body heat faster than adults, if you are taking them to areas where such rapid temperature changes can occur, make sure you know what you are doing and are completely prepared.

Altitude Sickness Acute Mountain Sickness or AMS occurs at high altitude and can be fatal. The lack of oxygen at high altitudes affects most people to some extent.

Even with acclimatisation you may still have trouble adjusting – headaches, nausea, dizziness, a dry cough, insomnia, breathlessness and loss of appetite are all signs to heed. Mild altitude problems will generally abate after a day or so but if the symptoms persist or become worse the only treatment is to descend – even 500 metres can help. Breathlessness, a dry, irritative cough (which may progress to the production of pink, frothy sputum), severe headache, loss of appetite, nausea, and sometimes vomiting are all danger signs. Increasing tiredness, confusion, and lack of coordination

PREVENTING ACUTE MOUNTAIN SICKNESS

Ascend slowly – have frequent rest days, spending two to three nights at each rise of 1,000 metres. If you reach a high altitude by trekking, acclimatisation takes place gradually and you are less likely to be affected than if you fly direct.

Drink extra fluids. The mountain air is dry and cold and moisture is lost as you breathe.

Eat light, high-carbohydrate meals for more energy.

Adults should avoid alcohol as it may increase the risk of dehydration.

Avoid sedatives.

and balance are real danger signs. Any of these symptoms individually, even just a persistent headache, can be a warning.

There is no hard and fast rule as to how high is too high: AMS has been fatal at altitudes of 3000 metres, although 3500 to 4500 metres is the usual range. It is always wise to sleep at a lower altitude than the greatest height reached during the day.

Again this is an illness which will affect children more quickly and seriously than adults.

Motion Sickness Eating lightly before and during a trip will reduce the chances of motion sickness. If your children are prone to motion sickness try to find a place that minimises disturbance – near the wing on aircraft, close to midships on boats, near the centre on buses. Fresh air usually helps, reading or cigarette smoke doesn't.

Commercial antimotion-sickness preparations, which can cause drowsiness, have to be taken before the trip commences; when you're feeling sick it's too late. Ginger is a natural preventative and is available in capsule form.

Jet Lag Jet lag is experienced when you travel by air across more than three time zones (each time zone usually represents a one-hour time difference). It occurs because many of the functions of the human body (such as temperature, pulse rate and emptying of the bladder and bowels) are regulated by internal 24-hour cycles called circadian rhythms. When we travel long distances rapidly, our bodies take time to adjust to the 'new time' of our destination, and we may experience fatigue, disorientation, insomnia, anxiety, impaired concentration and loss of appetite. These effects will usually be gone within three days of arrival, but there are ways of minimising the impact of jet lag.

It takes children even longer to adjust to a new time zone, and you may have a few broken nights at the beginning. See the section on Changing Time Zones in the Getting There & Away chapter for details on how to cope with jet-lag and how it affects kids.

AVOIDING JET LAG

Rest for a couple of days prior to departure; try to avoid late nights and last-minute dashes for travellers' cheques, passport etc.

Try to select flight schedules that minimise sleep deprivation; arriving late in the day means you can go to sleep soon after you arrive. For very long flights, try to organise a stopover.

Avoid excessive eating (which bloats the stomach) and alcohol (which causes dehydration) during the flight. Instead, drink plenty of non-carbonated, non-alcoholic drinks such as fruit juice or water

Sit with children in the non-smoking section as cigarette smoke reduces the amount of oxygen in the cabin even further and causes greater fatigue.

Make yourself and your children comfortable by wearing loose-fitting clothes and perhaps bringing an eye mask and ear plugs to help you sleep.

Infectious Diseases

Diarrhoea A change of water, food or climate can all cause the runs; diarrhoea caused by contaminated food or water is more serious. Totally breastfed babies are normally safe but despite all your precautions older children may still have a bout of mild travellers' diarrhoea. A few rushed toilet trips with no other symptoms is not indicative of a serious problem. Moderate diarrhoea, involving half-a-dozen loose movements in a day, is more of a nuisance. However, any diarrhoea in babies and small children should be considered serious.

Dehydration is the main danger with any diarrhoea, particularly for children where dehydration can occur quickly. Fluid replacement remains the mainstay of management. Weak black tea with a little sugar, soda water, or soft drinks allowed to go flat and diluted 50% with water are all good. With severe diarrhoea a rehydrating solution is necessary to replace minerals and salts. Commercially available ORS (oral rehydration salts) is very useful; add the contents of one sachet to a litre of boiled or bottled water. In an emergency you can make up a solution of eight teaspoons of sugar to a litre of boiled water and provide salted cracker biscuits at the same time. Your children should be kept on a bland diet as they recover.

Lomotil or Imodium can be used to bring relief from the symptoms of diarrhoea, although they do not actually cure the problem. Only use these drugs if absolutely necessary: when you *must* travel. For children it is preferable to use

---

ANTIBIOTICS FOR DIARRHOEA

Use antibiotics for the treatment of diarrhoea in the following intances:

Watery diarrhoea with blood and mucous. (Gut-paralysing drugs like Imodium or Lomotil should be avoided in this situation.)

Watery diarrhoea with fever and lethargy.

Persistent diarrhoea for more than five days.

Severe diarrhoea, if it is logistically difficult to stay in one place.

Imodium, but under all circumstances fluid replacement is the main message. Do not use these drugs if the child has a high fever or is severely dehydrated.

Antbiotics may sometimes be indicated. See the information box above.

The recommended drugs (adults only) would be either norfloxacin (Noroxin) 400 mg twice daily for three days or ciprofloxacin (Ciproxin) 500 mg twice daily for three days.

The drug bismuth subsalicylate has also been used successfully. It is not available in Australia. The dosage for adults is two tablets or 30 mls and for children it is one tablet or 10 mls. This dose can be repeated every 30 minutes to one hour, with no more than eight doses in a 24-hour period.

The drug of choice for children would be co-trimoxazole (Bactrim, Septrin, Resprim) with dosage dependent on weight. A three-day course is also given.

Ampicillin has been recommended in the past and may still be an alternative.

Giardiasis The parasite which causes this intestinal disorder is present in contaminated water. The symptoms are stomach cramps, nausea, a bloated stomach, watery, foul-smelling diarrhoea and frequent gas.

Giardiasis can appear several weeks after you have been exposed to the parasite. The symptoms may disappear for a few days and then return, continuing like this for several weeks.

Tinidazole, known as Fasigyn, or metronidazole (Flagyl) are the drugs recommended for treatment. Either can be used in a single treatment dose. Flagyl also comes in suspension form which is much more convenient when treating toddlers.

Dysentery This serious illness is caused by contaminated food or water and is characterised by severe diarrhoea, often with blood or mucus in the stool. There are two kinds of dysentery: bacillary and amoebic.

Bacillary dysentery is characterised by a high fever and rapid onset; headache, vomiting and stomach pains are also symptoms. It generally does not last longer than a week, but it is highly contagious.

Amoebic dysentery is often more gradual in the onset of symptoms, with cramping abdominal pain and vomiting less likely; fever may not be present. It is not a self-limiting disease: it will persist until treated and can recur and cause long-term health problems.

A stool test is necessary to diagnose which kind of dysentery you have, so you should seek medical help urgently. In case of an emergency the drugs norfloxacin or ciprofloxacin can be used as presumptive treatment for bacillary dysentery, and metronidazole (Flagyl) for amoebic dysentery.

For bacillary dysentery, norfloxacin 400 mg twice daily for seven days or ciprofloxacin 500 mg twice daily for seven days are the recommended dosages.

If you're unable to find either of these drugs then a useful alternative is co-trimoxazole 160/800 mg (Bactrim, Septrin, Resprim) twice daily for seven days. This is a sulfa drug and must not be used in people with a known sulfa allergy. In the case of children the drug co-trimoxazole is a reasonable first line treatment.

For amoebic dysentery, the recommended adult dosage of metronidazole (Flagyl) is one 400 mg capsule three times daily for five to seven days. Children aged between eight and 12-years-old should have half the adult dose; the dosage for younger children is one-third the adult dose.

An alternative to Flagyl is Fasigyn, taken as a two gram single daily dose for three days. For children under 12-years-old the dosage is 50 mg per kg of body weight, so if your child weighs 20 kg the dose is 1000 mg (one gram) per day. Adults should avoid alcohol during treatment and for 48 hours afterwards.

Cholera Cholera vaccination is not very effective. The bacteria responsible for this disease are waterborne, so that attention to the rules of eating and drinking should protect the traveller.

Outbreaks of cholera are generally widely reported, so you can avoid such problem areas. The disease is characterised by a sudden onset of acute diarrhoea with 'rice water' stools, vomiting, muscular cramps, and extreme weakness. You need medical help – but treat for dehydration, which can be extreme, and if there is an appreciable delay in getting to hospital begin taking tetracycline.

The adult dose is 250 mg four times daily. For children eight to 12-years-old the dose is 25 mg per kg of body weight four times daily. It is not recommended for children aged eight years or under nor for pregnant women. An alternative drug is ampicillin, for which the adult dose is 250 mg four times a day. Children aged eight to 12-years-old should take half the adult dosage, children under eight-years-old one-third the adult dosage.

Remember that while antibiotics might kill the bacteria, it is a toxin produced by the bacteria which causes the massive fluid loss. Fluid replacement is by far the most important aspect of treatment.

Viral Gastroenteritis This is caused not by bacteria but, as the name suggests, by a virus. It is characterised by stomach cramps, diarrhoea, and sometimes by vomiting and/or a slight fever. All you can do is rest and drink lots of fluids.

Hepatitis Hepatitis is a general term for inflammation of the liver. There are many causes of this condition: drugs, alcohol and infections are but a few.

The discovery of new strains has led to a virtual alphabet soup, with hepatitis A, B, C, D, E and a rumoured G. These letters identify specific agents that cause viral hepatitis. Viral hepatitis is an infection of the liver, which can lead to jaundice (yellow skin), fever, lethargy and digestive problems. It can have no symptoms at all, with the infected person not knowing that they have the disease. Travellers shouldn't be too paranoid about this apparent proliferation of hepatitis strains; hep C, D, E and G are fairly rare (so far) and following the same precautions as for A and B should be all that's necessary to avoid them.

Viral hepatitis can be divided into two groups on the basis of how it is spread. The first route of transmission is via contaminated food and water, and the second route is via blood and bodily fluids. The following types of hepatitis are spread by contaminated food and water:

Hepatitis A (HAV) This is a very common disease in most countries, especially those with poor standards of sanitation. Most people in developing countries are infected as children; they often don't develop symptoms, but do develop life-long immunity. The disease poses a real threat to the traveller, as people are unlikely to have been exposed to hepatitis A in developed countries.

The symptoms are fever, chills, headache, fatigue, feelings of weakness and aches and pains, followed by loss of appetite, nausea, vomiting, abdominal pain, dark urine, light coloured faeces,

jaundiced skin and the whites of the eyes may turn yellow. In some cases you may feel unwell, tired, have no appetite, experience aches and pains and be jaundiced. You should seek medical advice, but in general there is not much you can do apart from resting, drinking lots of fluids, eating lightly and avoiding fatty foods. People who have had hepatitis must forego alcohol for six months after the illness, as hepatitis attacks the liver and it needs that amount of time to recover.

The routes of transmission are via contaminated water, shellfish contaminated by sewerage, or foodstuffs sold by food handlers with poor standards of hygiene.

Taking care with what you eat and drink can go a long way towards preventing this disease. But this is a very infectious virus, so if there is any risk of exposure, additional cover is highly recommended. This cover comes in two forms: Gammaglobulin and Havrix. Gammaglobulin is an injection where you are given the antibodies for hepatitis A, which provide immunity for a limited time. Havrix is a vaccine, where you develop your own antibodies, which gives lasting immunity.

Hepatitis E (HEV) This is a very recently discovered virus, of which little is yet known. It appears to be rather common in developing countries, generally causing mild hepatitis, although it can be very serious in pregnant women.

Care with water supplies is the only current prevention, as there are no specific vaccines for this type of hepatitis. At present it doesn't appear to be too great a risk for travellers.

The following strains are spread by contact with blood and bodily fluids:

Hepatitis B (HBV) This is also a very common disease, with almost 300 million chronic carriers in the world. Hepatitis B, which used to be called serum hepatitis, is spread through contact with infected blood, blood products or bodily fluids, for example through sexual contact, unsterilised needles and blood transfusions. Other risk situations include having a shave or tattoo in a local shop, or having your ears pierced. The symptoms of type B are much the same as type A except that they are more severe and may lead to irreparable liver damage or even liver cancer. Although there is no treatment for hepatitis B, a cheap and effective vaccine is available; the only problem is that for long-lasting cover you need a six-month course. The immunisation schedule requires two injections at least a month apart followed by a third dose five months after the second. Persons who should receive a hepatitis B vaccination include anyone who anticipates contact with blood or other bodily secretions, either as a health-care worker or through sexual contact with the local population, particularly those who intend to stay in the country for a long period of time.

Hepatitis C (HCV) This is another recently defined virus. It is a concern because it seems to lead to liver disease more rapidly than hepatitis B.

The virus is spread by contact with blood – usually via contaminated transfusions or shared needles. Avoiding these is the only means of prevention, as there is no available vaccine.

Hepatitis D (HDV) Often referred to as the 'Delta' virus, this infection only occurs in chronic carriers of hepatitis B. It is transmitted by blood and bodily fluids. Again there is no vaccine for this virus, so avoidance is the best prevention. The risk to travellers is certainly limited.

Typhoid Typhoid fever is another gut infection that travels the faecal-oral route, which means that contaminated water and food are responsible. Vaccination against typhoid is not totally effective and it is one of the most dangerous infections, so medical help must be sought.

In its early stages typhoid resembles many other illnesses: your child may feel like they have a bad cold or flu on the way, as early symptoms are a headache, a sore throat, and a fever which rises a little each day until it is around 40°C or more. The patient's pulse is often slow relative to the degree of fever present and gets slower as the fever rises – unlike a normal fever where the pulse increases. There may also be vomiting, diarrhoea or constipation.

In the second week the high fever and slow pulse continue and a few pink spots may appear on the body. Trembling, delirium, weakness, weight loss and dehydration are other symptoms. If there are no further complications, the fever and other symptoms will slowly go during the third week. However you must get medical help before this because pneumonia (acute infection of the lungs) or peritonitis (perforated bowel) are common complications, and because typhoid is very infectious.

The fever should be treated by keeping the child cool and dehydration should also be watched for.

The drug of choice is ciprofloxacin (Ciproxin) at a dose of one gram daily for 14 days. It is quite expensive and may not be available. The alternative, chloramphenicol, has been the mainstay of treatment for many years. In many countries it is still the recommended antibiotic, but there are fewer side affects with ampicillin. The adult dosage is two 250 mg capsules, four times a day. Children aged between eight and 12-years-old should have half the adult dosage, younger children should have one-third the adult dose.

People who are allergic to penicillin should not be given ampicillin.

Worms These parasites are most common in rural, tropical areas and a stool test when you return home is not a bad idea. They can be present on unwashed vegetables or in undercooked meat and you can pick them up by walking in bare feet. Infestations may not show up for some time and although they are generally not serious, they can cause severe health problems if left untreated. A stool test is necessary to pinpoint the problem and medication is often available over the counter.

Children often get worms, even at home, so it may be a good idea to carry some worm treatment and pay attention if your children complain of an 'itchy bottom', are very restless while sleeping, wake up often, or go off their food. Talk to your doctor about it before you go.

Tetanus This potentially fatal disease is found in undeveloped tropical areas. It is difficult to treat but is preventable with immunisation. Tetanus occurs when a wound becomes infected by a germ which lives in the faeces of animals or people, so clean all cuts, punctures or animal bites. Tetanus is also known as lockjaw, and the first symptom may be discomfort in swallowing, or stiffening of the jaw and neck; this is followed by painful convulsions of the jaw and whole body.

Rabies Rabies is found in many countries and is caused by a bite or scratch by an infected animal. Dogs, monkeys, cats and bats are noted carriers. Any bite, scratch or even lick from a warm-blooded, furry animal should be cleaned immediately and thoroughly. Scrub with soap and running water, and then clean with an alcohol solution. If there is any possibility that the animal is infected medical help should be sought immediately. Even if the animal is not rabid, all bites should be treated seriously as they can become infected or can result in tetanus.

A rabies vaccination is available and should be considered in high-risk situations – if you intend to explore caves where there are bats, or work with animals. Make it clear to your children that animals are to be left alone.

Meningococcal Meningitis Sub-Saharan Africa is considered the 'meningitis belt' and the meningitis season occurs at the time most people would be attempting the overland trip across the Sahara – the northern winter before the rains come. Other areas which have recurring epidemics are Mongolia, Vietnam, Brazil, the Nile Valley and Nepal.

Trekkers to rural areas of Nepal should be particularly careful, as the disease is spread through coughs and sneezes by people who may not be aware that they are carriers. Lodges in the hills where travellers spend the night are prime spots for the spread of infection.

This very serious disease attacks the brain and can be fatal. A scattered, blotchy rash, fever, severe headache, sensitivity to light and neck stiffness which prevents forward bending of the head are the first symptoms. Death can occur within a few hours, so immediate treatment is important.

Treatment is large doses of penicillin given intravenously, or, if that is not possible, intramuscularly. Vaccination is expensive but offers good protection for over a year, but you should also check for reports of current epidemics.

Tuberculosis (TB) Although this disease is widespread in many developing countries, it is not a serious risk to travellers. Young children are more susceptible than adults and vaccination is a sensible precaution for children under 12-years-old travelling for extended periods in endemic areas. TB is commonly spread by coughing or by ingesting unpasteurised dairy products from infected cows. Milk that has been boiled is safe to drink; the fermentation of milk to make yoghurt or cheese also kills the bacilli.

Bilharzia Bilharzia is carried in fresh water by minute worms. The larvae infect certain varieties of freshwater snails, found in rivers, streams, lakes and particularly behind dams. The worms multiply and are eventually discharged into the water surrounding the snails.

The worm enters through the skin, and the first symptom may be tingling and sometimes a light rash around the area where it entered. The larvae attach themselves to your intestines or bladder, where they produce large numbers of eggs. Weeks later, when the worm is busy producing eggs, a high fever may develop. A general feeling of being unwell may be the first symptom; once the disease is established abdominal pain and blood in the urine are other signs.

Avoiding swimming or bathing in water where bilharzia is present is the main method of preventing the disease. Even deep water can be infected. If you do get wet, dry off quickly and dry your clothes as well. Seek medical attention if you have been exposed to the disease and tell the doctor your suspicions, as bilharzia in the early stages can be confused with malaria or typhoid. If you cannot get medical help immediately, praziquantel (Biltricide) is the recommended treatment. The recommended dosage is 40 mg/kg in divided doses over one day. Niridazole is an alternative drug.

Diphtheria Diphtheria can be a skin infection or a more dangerous throat infection. It is spread by contaminated dust contacting the skin or by the inhalation of infected cough or sneeze droplets. Frequent washing and keeping the skin dry will help prevent skin infection. A vaccination is available to prevent the throat infection.

Sexually Transmitted Diseases

Sexual contact with an infected sexual partner spreads these diseases. While abstinence is the only 100% preventative, using condoms is also effective. Gonorrhoea and syphilis are the most common of these diseases; sores, blisters or rashes around the genitals, discharges or pain when urinating are common symptoms. Symptoms may be less marked or not observed at all in women. Syphilis symptoms eventually disappear completely but the disease continues and can cause severe problems in later years. The treatment of gonorrhoea and syphilis is by antibiotics.

There are numerous other sexually transmitted diseases, for most of which effective treatment is available. However, there is no cure for herpes and there is also currently no cure for AIDS.

HIV/AIDS HIV, the Human Immunodeficiency Virus, may develop into AIDS, Acquired Immune Deficiency Syndrome. HIV is a major problem in many countries. Any exposure to blood, blood products or bodily fluids may put the individual at risk. In many developing countries transmission is predominantly through heterosexual sexual activity. This is quite different from industrialised countries where transmission is mostly through contact between homosexual or bisexual males, or via contaminated needles shared by IV drug users. Apart from abstinence, the most effective preventative is always to practise safe sex using condoms. It is impossible to detect the HIV-positive status of an otherwise healthy-looking person without a blood test.

HIV/AIDS can also be spread through infected blood transfusions; most developing countries cannot afford to screen blood for transfusions. It can also be spread by dirty needles – vaccinations, acupuncture, tattooing and ear or nose piercing can potentially be as dangerous as intravenous drug use if the equipment is not clean. If you do need an injection, ask to see the syringe unwrapped in front of you, or better still, take a needle and syringe pack with you overseas – it is a cheap insurance package against infection with HIV.

Fear of HIV infection should never preclude treatment for serious medical conditions. Although there may be a risk of infection, it is very small indeed.

Insect-Borne Diseases

Malaria This serious disease is spread by mosquitos. If you are travelling in endemic areas it is extremely important to take malarial prophylactics. Symptoms include headaches, fever, chills and sweating which may subside and recur. Without treatment malaria can develop more serious, potentially fatal effects.

Antimalarial drugs do not prevent you from being infected but kill the parasites during a normal stage in their development.

There are a number of different types of malaria. The one of most concern is falciparum malaria. This is responsible for the very serious cerebral malaria. Falciparum is the predominant form in many malaria prone areas of the world, including Africa, South-East Asia and Papua New Guinea. Contrary to popular belief cerebral malaria is not a new strain.

The problem in recent years has been the emergence of increasing resistance to commonly used antimalarials like chloroquine, maloprim and proguanil. Newer drugs such as mefloquine (Lariam) and doxycycline (Vibramycin, Doryx) are often recommended for

MALARIA PREVENTION

Primary prevention must always be in the form of mosquito avoidance measures. The mosquitoes that transmit malaria bite from dusk to dawn, and during that time travellers are advised to:

- wear light coloured clothing.
- wear long pants and long sleeved shirts; for babies you can get cotton sleeping bags which have arms and neck holes but are sewn across the bottom like a bag.
- use mosquito repellents containing the compound DEET on exposed areas.
- avoid highly scented perfumes or aftershave.
- use a mosquito net.
- where possible get a room with a fan as mosquitoes don't like the movement of the air and if your bed is positioned under the fan they will stay away.
- carry an insect spray, mosquito coils or a vaporiser.

While no antimalarial is 100% effective, taking the most appropriate drug significantly reduces the risk of contracting the disease.

No one should ever die from malaria. It can be diagnosed by a simple blood test. Symptoms range from fever, chills and sweating, headache and abdominal pains to a vague feeling of ill-health, so seek examination immediately if there is any possibility of malaria.

chloroquine and multi-drug resistant areas. Expert advice should be sought from your doctor, as there are many factors to consider when deciding on the type of antimalarial medication, including the area to be visited, the risk of exposure to malaria-carrying mosquitoes, your children's current medical condition and their ages. It is also important to discuss the side-effect profile of the medication, so you can work out some level of risk versus benefit ratio. It is also very important to be sure of the correct dosage of the medication prescribed. Some people inadvertently have taken weekly medication (chloroquine) on a daily basis, with disastrous effects. While discussing dosages for prevention of malaria, it is often advisable to include the dosages required for treatment, especially if your trip is through a high-risk area that would isolate you from medical care.

Malaria is curable, as long as the traveller seeks medical help when symptoms occur. Contrary to popular belief, once a traveller contracts malaria they do not have it for life. One of the parasites may lie dormant in the liver but can be eradicated using a specific medication.

It may be worth taking your own mosquito net as a preventative measure, although you may not always find somewhere to hang it. If your child wakes up a lot in the night, you may find it hard to remember, in your befuddled state, to make sure the net is closed properly when you fall back into bed. Of course this is not so much a problem if you are sleeping under the net with your child. In areas with severe mosquito problems hotels often provide mosquito nets, 'flea bags' as Kieran called them in Africa.

I close up the room (as much as possible) and spray it each evening before dinner. When we come back the smell, and hopefully any residue, has dispersed and any mosquitoes are dead.

Mosquito coils are useful; but buy them when you arrive as they are very fragile. I always burn a coil in the bathroom overnight, unless it is well sealed, as mosquitoes congregate where it is damp. Vaporisers are only useful where there is electric power. These small, portable gadgets vaporise insecticide tablets. They don't produce smells or smoke but the insecticide is still released into the air. If you buy one before you leave home check that it uses the appropriate voltage and you have the right adaptor.

It's a good idea to carry some preparation which will take the itch or sting out of insect bites. There are some good preparations and antihistamine creams which work well. If your child has an allergic reaction when bitten (Kieran has a strong allergic reaction; the bites swell up quite alarmingly and look very inflamed) you may find an antihistamine medication will help. Ask your doctor or pharmacist before you leave home, although many of these preparations are available over the counter in pharmacies everywhere. Some brand names are Sudafed, Actifed, Phenergan or Benadryl.

I find that when Kieran has one or two severe bites he will wake up crying and scratching several times during the night. This will occur for up to three nights when the bite finally fades. I now have a going-to-bed routine where I check Kieran after his bath, put calamine lotion on any bites and if he has some very large ones which have been bothering him during the day, I give him the required amount of antihistamine. It reduces his reaction to the bite and helps him to sleep.

Sleeping Sickness

In parts of tropical Africa tsetse flies can carry trypanosomiasis or sleeping sickness. They pass it on by biting large mammals and are responsible for the lack of horses and cows in some areas.

The tsetse fly is about twice the size of a housefly and recognisable by the scissor-like way it folds its wings when at rest. The flies are attracted to large moving objects (like safari buses) to perfume or aftershave, and to dark colours. Only a small proportion of tsetse flies carry the disease but it is best to avoid being bitten. Swelling at the site of the bite, five or more days after being bitten, is the first sign of infection; followed within two to three weeks by fever. The illness is serious but responds well to medical attention. There is no immunisation against sleeping sickness.

Dengue Fever

There is no prophylactic available for this mosquito-spread disease; the main preventative measure is to avoid being bitten. A sudden onset of fever, headaches and severe joint and muscle pains are the first signs of infection, followed by a rash on the trunk of the body that spreads to the limbs and face. After a further few days, the fever will subside and recovery will begin. Serious complications are not common.

Yellow Fever

This disease is endemic in many African and South American countries between 15° north and 15° south of the equator. This viral disease is transmitted to humans by mosquitoes. The initial symptoms are fever, headache, abdominal pain and vomiting. There may appear to be a brief recovery before the disease progresses to more severe complications, including liver failure. There is no medical treatment apart from keeping the fever down and avoiding dehydration, but yellow fever vaccination gives good protection for 10 years. Vaccination is an entry requirement for some countries, predominantly for those travellers coming from an infected area. Vaccination is not recommended for children less than one year old.

Chaga's Disease

In remote rural areas of South and Central America this parasitic disease is transmitted by a bug which hides in crevices and palm fronds and often takes up residence in the thatched roofs of huts. It comes out to feed at night. A hard, violet-coloured swelling appears at the site of the bite in about a week. Usually the body overcomes the disease unaided, but sometimes it continues and can eventually lead to death years later.

Chaga's disease can be treated in its early stages, but it is best to take preventative measures: avoid thatched-roof huts, sleep under a mosquito net, use insecticides and insect repellents and check for hidden insects.

Typhus

Typhus is spread by ticks, mites or lice. It begins as a bad cold, followed by a fever, chills, headache, muscle pains and a body rash. There is often a large, painful sore at the site of the bite and nearby lymph nodes are swollen and painful.

Tick typhus is spread by ticks. Trekkers in southern Africa may be at risk from cattle or wild animal ticks. Scrub typhus is spread by mites that feed on infected rodents and exists mainly in Asia and the Pacific Islands. You should take precautions if walking in rural areas in South-East Asia. Seek local advice on areas where ticks pose a danger and always check your skin carefully for ticks after walking in a danger area, such as a tropical forest. A strong insect repellent can help, and serious walkers in tick areas should consider having their boots and trousers impregnated with benzyl benzoate and dibutylphthalate.

Cuts, Bites & Stings

Cuts & Scratches Skin punctures can easily become infected in hot climates and may be difficult to heal. Treat any cut with an antiseptic such as Betadine. Where possible avoid bandages and Band-aids, which can keep wounds wet. Coral cuts are notoriously slow to heal, as the coral injects a weak venom into the wound. Avoid coral cuts by wearing shoes when walking on reefs, and clean any cut thoroughly with sodium peroxide if available.

Make it a general rule that all cuts and grazes, no matter how insignificant they seem, are treated with antiseptic as soon as possible. Tony and I both have experienced little scratches becoming infected wounds which took a very long time to heal. Tony actually had to have a penicillin injection, three months after the skin was broken, to cure what had been a tiny scratch.

Creams and ointments should not be used as these just keep the wound greasy and prevent it from healing. If infection does occur you could try an antibiotic powder, but check that it has not passed its expiry date. Local pharmacies or first aid centres can often treat cuts, scratches or minor wounds very competently. Bathing a wound in salt water helps to clean and sterilise a wound.

Bites & Stings Bee and wasp stings are usually painful rather than dangerous. Calamine lotion will give relief or ice packs will reduce the pain and swelling. There are some spiders with dangerous bites but antivenenes are usually available. Scorpion stings are notoriously painful and in Mexico can actually be fatal. Scorpions often shelter in shoes or clothing.

Certain cone shells found in Australia and the Pacific can sting dangerously or even fatally. Various fish and other sea creatures can either sting or bite dangerously, or are dangerous to eat. Again, local advice is the best suggestion.

Snakes To minimise your chances of being bitten always dress your child in boots or stout shoes, socks and long trousers when walking through undergrowth where snakes may be present. Warn your children not to put their hands into holes and crevices, and to be careful when collecting firewood.

Snake bites do not cause instant death

and antivenenes are usually available. Keep the victim calm and still, wrap the bitten limb tightly, as you would for a sprained ankle, and then attach a splint to immobilise it. Then seek medical help, if possible with the dead snake for identification. Don't attempt to catch the snake if there is even a remote possibility of being bitten again. Tourniquets and cutting the bite area to suck out the venom are now comprehensively discredited.

Jellyfish Use local advice to find out the best way of avoiding contact with these sea creatures with their stinging tentacles. The box jellyfish found in inshore waters around northern Australia during the summer months is potentially fatal, but stings from most jellyfish are simply rather painful. Dousing in vinegar will de-activate any stingers which have not 'fired'. Calamine lotion, antihistamines and analgesics may reduce the reaction and relieve the pain.

Bedbugs & Lice Bedbugs live in various places, but particularly in dirty mattresses and bedding. Spots of blood on bedclothes or on the wall around the bed can be read as a suggestion to find another hotel. Bedbugs leave itchy bites in neat rows. Calamine lotion may help.

All lice cause itching and discomfort. They make themselves at home in your children's hair (head lice) or clothing (body lice). They are caught through direct contact with infected people or by sharing combs, clothing and the like. Lots of children in the West bring head lice home from school and they are even more prevalent in developing countries – how often do you see people grooming each other's hair and searching for lice? Your children's contact with local children may well be closer than your own contact with the locals so be prepared. You may think it is a good idea to carry an appropriate treatment shampoo with you. Infected clothing should be washed in very hot water.

Leeches & Ticks Leeches may be present in damp rainforest conditions. Trekkers often get them on their legs or in their boots; they attach themselves to the skin to suck blood. Salt or a lighted cigarette end will make them fall off. Do not pull them off, as the bite is then more likely to become infected. An insect repellent may keep them away. Vaseline, alcohol or oil will also persuade a tick to let go. You should always check your body if you have been walking through a tick-infested area, as they can spread typhus.

Women's Health

Gynaecological Problems Poor diet, lowered resistance due to the use of antibiotics for stomach upsets, vaginal changes during pregnancy and even contraceptive pills can lead to vaginal infections when travelling in hot climates. Keeping the genital area clean, and wearing skirts or loose-fitting trousers and cotton underwear will help to prevent infections.

Yeast infections, characterised by a rash, itch and discharge, can be treated with a vinegar or lemon-juice douche, or with yoghurt. Nystatin suppositories are the usual medical prescription. Trichomoniasis is a more serious infection; symptoms are a discharge and a burning sensation when urinating. Male sexual partners must also be treated, and if a vinegar-water douche is not effective medical attention should be sought. Metronidazole (Flagyl) is the prescribed drug for treatment.

Pregnancy Most miscarriages occur during the first three months of pregnancy, so this is the most risky time to travel as far as your own health is concerned. See the Travelling Pregnant chapter for additional information.

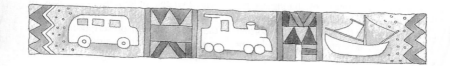

USA, AFRICA & NEPAL

*Kieran Wheeler
has been travelling
with his parents,
Tony & Maureen,
and sister Tashi all
of his 12 years.*

ALL MY LIFE I HAVE TRAVELLED. Sometimes it is fun and sometimes it is a fate worse than death: you have to take that chance. Some places you go to have none of the food you like and the accommodation is less then five-star, but half the time travelling is a great adventure. I have experienced thrills in many places, but the one that I remember best is Africa.

The main attraction of Africa is the safari: you go by bus into the home of many different animals and see lion cubs and everything you would expect to see in the heart of Africa. At night you camp in tents. When you wake up, you meet a campfire with breakfast ready for an army, which is exactly what we are; an army waiting to get on the bus and trek off. One night when one of the cooks was settling down for bed a big elephant smelled the pineapples in the tent and decided to take them and nearly picked up the cook!

In Africa, you will often be in a situation were you have to bargain – it's lots of fun. I used to love bargaining and I was quite good at it (if I may say so myself), so I'll give you a little tip: if you are trying to buy something for a certain price and the man you want to buy it off suggests a higher price say 'no deal' and walk off; half the time he'll say 'OK' and go back to the price you wanted.

Another place that really stands out was America. I love just about everything about it, especially the sport. I am a real NBA basketball fan and I actually went to one match which was a lot of fun. They have a huge score board hanging down from the roof and they show lots of funny cartoons on it.

In Las Vegas we went to a fantastic show called *Mystere*. There are no animals in it and I think that's a great thing. Instead it had acrobats who did some really

travel stories

fantastic tricks. We stayed in a fantastic resort called the Mirage and at night a fake volcano erupts every fifteen minutes. It is definitely a sight worth seeing! In another resort there was a pirate ship and a galleon with actors. Every hour they would go into battle and the pirates would always win and the great galleon would sink. There was also a resort called the Excalibur where every fifteen minutes a mechanical dragon would fight a mechanical Merlin. The food in Las Vegas was also terrific, which surprised Mum because she thought it would be tacky.

> **'The food in Las Vegas was also terrific, which surprised Mum because she thought it would be tacky. '**

I also liked Chicago a lot. I liked the food and the resorts and the shops and their basketball team. C'mon the bulls! I saw a baseball game here that I really enjoyed.

Another place that is on the top of my list is Nepal. As in Africa, I loved the safari, but the one in Nepal is different to those in Africa. Instead of seeing the animals from a bus you see them from the top of an elephant! It's a lot of fun to be way up on top of that great big elephant. At night you sleep in bunks and it is a little nicer than the tents, but you don't see as many animals as you do in Africa.

Another highlight of Nepal is the trek: each day you walk for about five, six or even seven hours, then at night you settle down in your tent. We once went on a trek with some family friends. The two main friends my age are Gigi and Bea Clarke. In the evenings we always played together and climbed hills and everything. One night we sat on a wall watching two bulls having a fight when suddenly they charged us; we didn't notice that there was a ten-foot drop on the other side of the wall and just tumbled backwards, landing on our backs: we laughed ourselves silly for the next half-hour.

Another great time was when we had just finished putting up our tents. The

travel stories

campsite was at the top of a massive hill, but instead of going downwards on a slope like a normal hill it went down in little staircase steps, each about 1.5 metres high. We decided to climb to the bottom of the hill and then climb back up step by step.

When we got to the bottom we saw a bunch of Nepalese kids who started to follow us. We decided they were American mountaineers trying to beat us to the top of Mt Everest and started to climb with the kids laughing and chasing after us. We got halfway up the mountain and realised that Gigi was missing; kidnapped by the Americans. We found him under a tree talking to them and told him that he'd been kidnapped and not to talk, but run. So we pelted up Mt Everest with the Americans in hot pursuit. In the end we won but gave the Americans three cheers, which they thought was hilarious. Then we poured the news out to our parents that we had beaten the Americans.

Kieran Wheeler

NEW ZEALAND

Kate Cody flew to New Zealand for a family wedding with Jackson when he was 18 months old.

WHEN MY COUSIN SARAHJANE DECIDED TO GET MARRIED, in the dead of winter, in Wellington, New Zealand, I knew that Jackson and I would be travelling to the wedding by ourselves because it was not exotic enough to meet the criterion for a 'family' holiday. The flight would only take four hours and there would be relatives to meet me at the other end so I gambled that I could survive a flight in the company of my eighteen-month-old son.

Fortunately, as soon as the seatbelt light went off he climbed straight into the lap of the quiet, elderly, turbanned Indian bloke sitting behind us. I tried to convince Jackson to return to his own seat but instead of cheerful cooperation I got the rigid body routine. When the genial passenger said that Jackson could stay with him I couldn't believe my luck: I might read a magazine and eat a meal after all. Maybe my fellow passengers wouldn't realise that the boisterous climbing midget had come aboard with me? Jackson came back to check on me occasionally and, reassured that I was still there, went straight back to his friend with my blessing.

I was staying in the same hotel as all the other relatives who were gathering for the wedding, so help was on hand. And I had cooking facilities in the room and a couple of cans of Baked Beans in case Jackson wouldn't eat anything else. Even though he was weaned by now, the strange surroundings were enough to ensure that he woke several times each night. And while the easiest thing seemed to be to bring him into my bed his teeth grinding and constant wriggling did not help me get any sleep.

The big day arrived, but I actually saw very little of the wedding because I had to take Jackson out of the church to stop him from climbing into the choir stalls and tripping the photographer. While Sarahjane and Brian were making their vows I was wrestling Jackson out of the fountain in the courtyard outside the church.

I did manage to find some child-oriented activities where Jackson and I were not in opposition. He loved running up and down the hilly paths in the Botanic Gardens and feeding the ducks from the rickety wooden bridge. We climbed the massive statues of lions near the Beehive, New Zealand's parliamentary building, and smelled every rose in its garden. And even though it was raining the whole time we were at the beach house in Waikanae, I encouraged Jackson to go outside and play in the vain hope that he'd get rid of some of his excess energy before we moved to our final accommodation back in town.

> ' *What a perfect environment to take Jackson into, when telling a child his age not to touch is like saying not to breathe.* '

We stayed for a couple of days in Ngaio with my cousin Andrea, who keeps her flat so well ordered she verges on having an obsessive compulsive disorder. What a perfect environment to take Jackson into, when telling a child his age not to touch is like saying not to breathe. The racks of wine on the floor, the bowls of potpourri on the coffee table, and the remote control for the TV all had to be removed to about ceiling height for the duration of our stay. And, although I'd cleaned, Andrea found fingerprints to wipe for months after our stay.

I was relieved to get on the plane home. I had spent less than a week in Wellington with Jackson but I knew that the next time I went overseas I'd take his father along too, and I'd go somewhere where it didn't matter if he ran amok.

Katie Cody

MEXICO

James, Pauline, Michael (seven, pictured) & Bennie (five) Lyon lived for five months in Mexico while James worked on LP's Mexico guide.

IT HAD BEEN A LONG DRIVE SOUTH FROM THE TEXAS BORDER, through Chihuahua and Durango, to Zacatecas, an old mining town which is usually described as a colonial gem. Somewhere along the way, Mike and Bennie had figured that if there was a Mothers Day, and a Fathers Day, then there should also be a Kids Day. It would be a *special* day – when they would have cake and presents and be able to do whatever they wanted. I suffer from the parental delusion that my kids nearly always get what they want, and they want too much, but at the time it seemed that they had a point. In the last few days we had looked at several baroque cathedrals, two *Museos de la Revolución* and an archeological ruin which they weren't allowed to climb on, so it was about time we had a day doing what the kids wanted.

I was contemplating this as we entered Zacatecas, and I saw, stretched over the narrow winding street, a white banner with bright blue lettering – 'Di\a del Niño 1994'. In Mexico there is a fiesta or a holiday every other week and, by amazing coincidence, tomorrow was the Day of the Child. Excitedly I told the boys that their wish had been granted but they seemed sceptical – suspicious even. 'What are we actually going to do?' they asked, 'What will we get?' I had to admit that I didn't know what Kids Day entailed in Zacatecas, but I was sure it would be fun. They were sure I was making it up.

The next day, a Sunday, I enquired at the hotel and was told that it was indeed the Day of the Child. I asked what that entailed and the desk clerk said it was a special day for children, when they got sweets and presents and were allowed to do.

The church is very important in Mexico, as is the family and the midday meal, so I wasn't surprised that there were few public events that morning, but it was beautiful, bright and sunny, and as usual there were plenty of people on the streets. The Mexican kids were even more smartly dressed than usual, even for a Sunday, and they seemed extra bright and cheerful. Our boys wore crumpled shorts, travel-soiled sneakers and sweatshirts, and were extra grumpy as they sensed that everyone else was in party mood and they hadn't been invited. Also, we were making them *walk* again, and that wasn't *fun*. The first sign that they were willing to enjoy the day came as we reached a busy ice-cream shop, and they reminded us that Kids Day meant that we had to buy them *helados*.

> *The kids were unimpressed with the superb view, the small museum and the big bronze statues of revolutionary heroes, but they were happy to hang out in one of the souvenir and snack stalls.*

Thus mollified, our kids let us coax them along steep, twisting cobblestoned streets to the most incongruous tourist trap in town – a *teleférico* (cable car) which will take you several hundred metres up Cerro de la Bufa. The kids were unimpressed with the superb view, the small museum and the big bronze statues of revolutionary heroes, but they were happy to hang out in one of the souvenir and snack stalls. The owner was wonderfully indulgent as they blew the Indian whistles, handled the Aztec calendars and sorted through his mineral collection, though all we bought were a couple of *refrescos* (soft drinks). At home, Coca-Cola is a special treat, but in Mexico they nearly lived on the stuff. The cable car only cost 4 pesos (about US$1.30) per person per trip, but for the whole family it seemed like a lot, and I thought we could walk down the hill to save some money and do something different. The kids wouldn't hear of it – 'It's Kids Day', they said, 'and we don't want to walk'.

After a fun ride down in the cable car, the action was hotting up in town. A local radio station had set up an outdoor stage in one of the shady little *(plazuelas)*, and a couple of clowns were drawing shrieks of laughter from a crowd of the local niños. As a finale they flung handfuls of sweets into the flock, and even threw out small toys and kids clothing. With atypical adroitness, I snatched a flying yo-yo from the air and gave it to Bennie, who might have been impressed but wasn't letting on. Then all the kids lined up to get a slice of the huge pink cream cake which was being distributed from one of the ancient doorways. Our boys were slow to get in line but the Mexican mothers made sure they got their share – as visitors as well as kids they were entitled to special kindness, and perhaps they felt sorry for the poor little *gringos* who didn't seem to be quite in the spirit of the day.

As darkness fell we made it to the main plaza, where a brass band was just finishing a performance for kids, who danced and marched with style and spontaneity. A group of small boys kicked a soccer ball across the cobblestones, though it was an unforgiving surface and the stone seats at the sides were so low that only the most precise shot would score a goal. Mike and Bennie leapt into the game with an enthusiasm which was not matched by their limited experience of *futbol*. Soon they had both fallen several times, and felt frustration as the local lads skipped skilfully around them. But the home team was ever so kind and generous, stopping the game to help our kids up, passing the ball to them and encouraging them to shoot for goal.

When our boys finally sat down, tired and bruised, the others came over and spoke to us sympathetically. It was hard to follow their slangy street Spanish, but I got the idea. My kids needed to practise more – didn't they have their own

ball? I admitted that they didn't. There were concerned looks, and muttered exchanges in which the phrase 'Día del Niño' was repeated several times. The kids moved away, went into a huddle, and returned a couple of minutes later with an old *futbol*, worn to a suede finish but still hard and useable. It was, they said, *un regalo*. I was embarrassed and overwhelmed by their kindness – these were not wealthy kids – but it was a present, and we couldn't refuse. So we chatted a while, and they all signed the ball like they were a professional soccer team. And we signed their ball, and I drew a little map of Australia on it, to show where we came from. Did they know anything about Australia I asked. 'Sure', they said, 'Australia was in Group G, but was beaten by Argentina and wouldn't make it to the World Cup finals in the USA'. They really did feel sorry for us.

James Lyon

TUNISIA

***Ruth Armes
(pictured with
Rupert) & Rob
Gibson travelled to
Tunisia when their
son Rupert was 18
months old.***

CONTRARY TO ALL TRAVELLING EXPECTATIONS, we arrived in Tunisia in daylight and were able to find accommodation at leisure. Based on our experience of Turkey we had decided to abandon the cloth nappies and carry a bag of disposables, hoping that we could buy more if we ran out. The extra space this released in our backpack we filled with a bed-roll for Rupert. This proved over optimistic as he would invariably make his own way into our bed during the night.

Rupert was predominantly breastfed when we went to Turkey, now 18-months-old he wanted 'real' food, particularly at breakfast. We took a large bag of muesli and some dried milk, along with a selection of dehydrated food which we heated up on a spirit stove.

Many of Tunisia's towns have the old town in the centre surrounded by a heavily fortified wall. This central area is called the medina and is a labyrinth of narrow alleyways. Some are eerily deserted, whilst others are filled to capacity and more. With Rupert in a backpack it sometimes proved near impossible to make progress against the throng. He, however, remained unconcerned about the mayhem, though he undoubtedly took it all in for he unfailingly spotted cats, dogs and other furry creatures and pointed them out to us.

We quickly left the capital, Tunis, and moved on to the beach resort of Sousse. Here Rupert stunned the locals, who were dressed in thick coats, by playing in the sea (fully clothed) and running about on the beach naked. Sousse has very little to offer other than the beach and those Tunisians engaged in the tourist industry are rather aggressive in their determination to relieve you of your money. It was in the medina here that the first of several attempts was made on the contents of our purse.

' The bus company man took us in hand... he produced more tea and a large hookah. '

At El Jem, the site of a very impressive Roman colosseum, we spent a pleasant afternoon's sightseeing. Then we had a long wait for the train south to Sfax, a large modern city that held little interest for us once the medina had been explored. The bus company man said there was a bus leaving at midnight for the south and that we could buy tickets at 8 pm. We went to get dinner and returned at 8 pm to be told that we could not have tickets until 10 pm. Fortunately we had met some German students in the same predicament, so we sat in a cafe drinking sweet tea for a couple of hours. Returning at 10 pm we were told 'maybe 11'. At this point we were starting to wonder if the bus existed at all. The bus company man took us in hand. He had a little sentry box from which he produced more tea and a large hookah. Unfortunately, Rupert woke up around midnight so we had a fairly miserable time until we eventually caught our bus at 1.30 am. Once on the road he quickly fell asleep and so did we.

We arrived at the bus terminus in Kebili at 5.30 am. As we disembarked we spotted some *louages* (taxis which do a fixed route for a fixed price). We struggled over to these and drove through the dawn to our final destination, Douz, the gateway to the Sahara. We arrived at 6.30 am, found a hotel room and crashed out. Rupert had remained asleep throughout the remainder of the journey.

Douz was wonderful, no sneak thieves here, in fact people just wanted to give us things. That day we walked through the oasis out into the sand dunes. Rupert had a fun time playing in the ultra-fine sand and chasing scarab beetles. On the return journey we met a date farmer who showed us the wells from which he drew his water. In some places the water was only a metre below the surface of the sand.

That evening after lengthy negotiations we arranged a trip into the desert for the following day using a combination of Land Rovers and camels. Sadly we woke up to find a sandstorm blowing, so our trip had to be cancelled. The day after was the festival of Eid al Fitr, celebrating the end of Ramadan, and our need to head north again prevented us from staying any longer.

We made the 160-km journey across the great salt lakes to Tozeur just in time to be at the festival. This was a joyous occasion with young girls parading in their finery and young boys galloping recklessly through the streets on horse-back. This was very much a children's event with many stalls given over to selling toys.

> ### *'The knife went as straight as an arrow, clipped a glass and thudded into the waiter's groin. '*

Rupert is usually a little charmer when it comes to waiters. He is frequently carried out the back to be shown to the cooks, sisters, aunts, mother-in-laws, etc, and returns bearing gifts of fruit. Though such separation in England would bring on howls of anguish from him, somehow the easygoing attitude of the people reassured him. One night Rupert was sitting at the table playing with the cutlery when he suddenly hurled a knife across the table. The knife went as straight as an arrow, clipped a glass and thudded into the waiter's groin. Our embarrassment was acute. It took Rupert the best part of the meal to win the waiter back over and to charm an orange from the proprietor.

To the west of Tozeur, on the Algerian border, the desert turns into mountains. These are equally barren except for small pockets of greenery where water rises to the surface. We drove up there in a Land Rover to see some of the villages. The lushness of these little oases is in stark contrast to the parched surroundings. On the return journey Rupert slept despite the heat and the lurching of the vehicle. When he is older we'll have to tell him how he missed the herds of wild camels which populated the plains.

The next day we were badly caught out by torrential rain with a distinctly European temperature. We had to cross town, which in places was several feet under water, to catch a bus to Kairouan. The man in the grocer's store helped us construct waterproofs for Rupert out of plastic carrier bags, so although he remained reasonably dry we arrived at the bus station drenched. We then had to sit for five hours on a bus shivering.

Kairouan is a regional religious centre; it is reported that five visits here equals one to Mecca. Some of the older, lesser mosques, though not breathtaking, are very picturesque. Unfortunately the cold northerly wind dampened our enthusiasm for sightseeing. Our feelings for the place were further soured by the attention of the local pickpockets. Although we lost nothing such encounters temporarily dent your feeling of well being. We returned to the hotel, negotiated the hire of a paraffin heater and waited for the bus to Tunis.

On our last day we went to Carthage. The Romans put paid to the area ever

travel stories

being a sightseeing attraction when they flattened it in 146 BC. One of the benefits of travelling is that it helps you put into order all those half forgotten facts learnt in stuffy classrooms. Now Carthage to us is a real place on a map and the Punic Wars a point in time. Rupert is too young to remember all these places when he reaches school, but maybe pictures of him playing in the Saharan sands will make the place a bit more real.

Rob Gibson

TRAVELLING PREGNANT

The day before Tony and I left to research our guidebook to India, I discovered I was pregnant. Since I had known it was a possibility I had decided that I would continue with the trip, even though I had had a miscarriage a few months before. I did not feel that going to India would increase my chances of

miscarrying again because I knew the country well and was quite aware of what I was letting myself in for. I also knew how to minimise the hassles, I was healthy, I intended to be careful and beyond that I really wanted to go.

While I was quite aware that a child was going to radically change my life, I was not prepared to start compromising before it was even born! I knew that after the baby was born I would still want to travel, so I felt that travelling with this small internal passenger was an entirely appropriate beginning.

When to Travel

Miscarriage is not uncommon during the first trimester, and can occasionally lead to severe bleeding. However, the first three months may be the best time to travel in that you are not too big, you don't get quite so tired and you may be more able emotionally to handle the problems you encounter while travelling. Unless you suffer from 'morning sickness' you may not feel too much

different from 'normal' and really enjoy your trip!

The last three months should also be spent within reasonable distance of good medical care. A baby born as early as 24 weeks stands a chance of survival, but only in a good modern hospital. During the third trimester your greater size makes you most tired and uncomfortable.

Airlines have regulations regarding the last trimester of pregnancy when they can refuse to carry you. These rules differ for domestic and international flights and is based on the risk and expense of having to divert the flight if you go into labour prematurely while on board.

Pregnant women should avoid all unnecessary medication, but vaccinations and malarial prophylactics should still be taken where possible. Additional care should be taken to prevent illness and particular attention should be paid to diet and nutrition. Alcohol and nicotine, for example, should be avoided.

Preparing

Before you organise your trip read up on pregnancy and health. Find a sympathetic doctor, preferably one who has travelled or deals with travellers, and ask their advice. You need a doctor who knows about vaccinations and suitable medications for the illnesses you are likely to be exposed to.

135

Read about the countries you are going to and choose your route carefully. It is easier to travel pregnant in a country you have already visited, or if you are an experienced traveller. Ask yourself if you are prepared to take the responsibility (and the flak!) if things go wrong – the risk is yours.

Food

Almost anywhere you travel it is possible to get good, healthy food. However, travelling off-the-beaten-track you may find it difficult to maintain a balanced diet or, particularly in places like India, the food may be so overcooked that little nutrition remains. In many developing countries dairy foods are not always available so it may be difficult to keep your calcium intake up.

It is important to maintain a good diet, so I would suggest that you upgrade your standard of restaurant whenever you feel it is necessary. Try not to miss meals or wait too long between meals. Read up on food values and nutritional requirements so that you know which foods to eat and get as much eggs, fruit, legumes, nuts, tofu and yogurt as possible.

Chinese restaurants seem to be found in even the most remote places in developing countries and their food is generally good. In India, dhal (a good source of protein) is almost always served with meals, or you can also ask for it. An Indian *thali* of rice, dhal, vegetables and yoghurt is a well-balanced meal. Yoghurt *(dahi* or 'curd') is often available if you ask, and you can also drink it as *lassi*, a delicious fruit and yogurt concoction..

Vitamin Supplements

Carry multi-vitamins, iron tablets and calcium tablets, and check with your doctor or a health food store as to the most appropriate.

Other Considerations

Apart from the medical considerations, in the first three months of pregnancy you will be surprised at three things:

How hungry you get. Tony used to be amazed at my capacity for Indian food. No matter how tasteless or awful it was, I ate mine, Tony's and anyone else's. If you miss a meal due to travelling by train or bus or arriving late you may feel sick or even faint, so always carry something to eat with you, and snack on fruit, biscuits, peanuts – anything you can find to keep you going. You do need it.

How tired you get. Don't try to do all the things you did before you got pregnant. Take frequent rests. If you have one day of hard travel, have a day or two of rest and just plan to travel at a slower pace.

How often you will need to find a toilet. You will need to go to the toilet more often than you thought physically possible. It's wise to dress for quick and convenient toilet visits.

You may find that travelling on a bus or train for many hours at a stretch makes your back ache. I found taking off and landing by plane also caused my lower back to ache. I met a doctor who was on the same flight to Leh and asked her what might be causing this. She thought it was probably caused by changes in pressure, and since it hadn't caused any real problems so far, it was probably all right.

If you are prone to motion sickness,

you should consider trying to avoid it by limiting your trips on vehicles that make you sick, particularly if you actually vomit since it is not a good idea for pregnant women to be violently sick. Check with your doctor if there is a safe medication you can take to prevent motion sickness or try a capsule of ginger before you travel.

Really, you have to take the same precautions you would if you stayed at home. Just be aware of any extra problems that might arise, and be prepared to accept the responsibility if anything goes wrong!

HEALTH

Women travellers often find that their periods become irregular or even cease while they're on the road. Remember that a missed period in these circumstances doesn't necessarily indicate pregnancy.

There are health posts or Family Planning clinics in many urban centres in developing countries, where you can seek advice and have a urine test to determine whether or not you are pregnant.

Vaccinations

The first hassle is the vaccinations. Ideally, pregnant women should not take drugs nor be given 'live vaccines'. Of course, if you plan to travel to some areas you must have certain vaccinations and take anti-malarials. See the Health chapter for information on which vaccinations are safe for pregnant women.

If you are planning to become pregnant and you know you may be travelling,

TRAVEL TIPS...

If you are planning to become pregnant and you know you may be travelling, try to get all the immunisations you need before you get pregnant.

try to get all the immunisations you need before you get pregnant. Due to the limited periods of immunity afforded by many vaccinations this may not be practical, but at least consider it where possible.

Diarrhoea

Try not to take any unnecessary medication. If you get diarrhoea, try to clear it up with rest and a bland diet. If you can't get rid of it this way use a kaolin preparation (available from most chemists in the West). Lomotil is contraindicated in pregnancy. If you do want to carry something with you for diarrhoea check with your doctor first. I was extra careful when I was travelling in India during my first pregnancy and didn't get sick at all. Preventing diarrhoea is much better than taking medication to get rid of it when you are pregnant.

Malaria

This disease can pass from the mother through the placenta to the foetus. If a mother contracts malaria during pregnancy her baby can be born with malaria. A pregnant woman is likely to have malaria far more seriously than the non-pregnant.

Some anti-malarial drugs, in particular chloroquine, are considered safe to take during pregnancy but others may have known side-effects or may not yet be sufficiently tested. Get advice from your doctor or health authorities as to which drug is most suitable for you. The Health chapter gives the current thinking on malarials for pregnant women.

Minor Problems

Yeast and fungal infections, such as thrush, can be a problem for the pregnant woman. Infections of the vagina are common in pregnant women anywhere, but if you are travelling in the tropics the hot climate exacerbates the problem. Cotton underwear that is not tight-fitting is absolutely essential. Don't wear tight jeans or trousers; loose cotton dresses are better. Carry an anti-fungal cream or appropriate oral medication.

SRI LANKA

**Susan Forsyth &
John Noble
travelled to Sri
Lanka when
daughter Isabella
(pictured) was 18
months old & Jack
was four months
in utero.**

JOHN NOBLE AND I VISITED SRI LANKA for three months in 1992 to update the
LP *Sri Lanka – travel survival kit*. I was four-months-pregnant and we had
our 1½ year old daughter Isabella with us. We've also subsequently holidayed
there with both children. We started our research trip on the south-west coast at
Hikkaduwa then moved on to Kandy which became home base for Isabella and
I while John scurried around the island. We met up with John from time to time
and together visited Nuwara Eliya, Colombo, Negombo and Polonnaruwa. We
were all basically healthy for the whole time.

Sri Lanka, political turmoil aside, is a great place to travel with children and
increasingly many foreigners are doing it (we overheard one traveller remark
that Hikkaduwa is becoming a 'family' beach) which means that children are
catered for to some extent. As elsewhere in Asia, Sri Lankan people love children
who always receive a warm welcome, especially those with blonde hair. Sri
Lanka offers a wide range of landscapes and possible activities within a
relatively small area. The colour and movement of Asia alone provides an
endless source of entertainment for children. Watch Western children's eyes
boggle at the sight of a large group of orange-robed monks carrying big black
umbrellas.

Romping on beautiful tropical beaches is an obvious attraction. The common
sightings of elephants is another. You can combine beach and elephants with an
elephant ride along the sand at Hikkaduwa. In the hill country, picturesque
Kandy has a lake, a cool climate, the Temple of the Tooth, museums, a bustling
market and lovely swimming pools. Children will also be impressed by the
acrobatic performances and colourful costumes of Kandy dancers. Higher into

the hill country, surrounded by tea plantations, the quaint colonial town of Nuwara Eliya also offers delicious respite from the heat, and pony rides. Also in the hill country, Horton Plains makes for good hiking, viable with older children or babies in a backpack, and the chance of spotting a leopard. More wildlife can be seen in Yala National Park in the south-east. For a completely different experience, there's the ancient cities of the cultural triangle in the dry zone to the north of Kandy.

Of special interest to kids is the Pinnewala Elephant Orphanage, near Kegalle, 77 km from Colombo on the Colombo to Kandy road. It was set up to save abandoned or orphaned wild elephants. There are about 35 young elephants which roam freely around the sanctuary (although controlled by their keepers). You can watch them bathing or being fed milk from enormous baby's bottles. Isabella was spellbound.

I had responsibility for the Kandy update. I researched the town mostly on foot pushing Isabella in a stroller but, when the hills got too much for my increasing bulk, we jumped into a three-wheeler ('bumpy car' to Isabella). As I hadn't been able to afford to ride in a three-wheeler when I was a volunteer lecturer near Kandy in 1986, I really enjoyed this mode of transport, though one trip on a dirt road almost brought on contractions. We spent the late afternoons at one of Kandy's many beautifully-sited swimming pools.

Carving at entrance to Temple of the Tooth, Kandy

Sri Lankan bus travel is tedious and cramped. Travel with children on local buses is almost out of the question except on short trips with a daypack and a stroller. We managed local buses from Hikkaduwa to Galle or Unawatuna, Colombo to Negombo, and around Kandy but, on longer hauls, there was simply not enough room for all our gear and my big belly. So, we hired a van and driver for long trips.

> ' *...there was simply not enough room for all our gear and my big belly. So, we hired a van and driver for long trips.* '

We did use trains several times, mainly for the scenic two-hour trip between Kandy and Colombo but also for our initial trip to Hikkaduwa from Colombo. Kandy to Colombo by train with kids is fine but the south coast route is not recommended as only 2nd class is available which means awful toilets, probably no seats and a good chance of parting with your luggage.

Disposable nappies are available at least in Colombo, Kandy and Hikkaduwa if you find these more convenient than cloth nappies. Baby cots are rare but we did find one at a middle-range hotel in Hikkaduwa and another at the *Galle Face Hotel* in Colombo (the large air-con rooms there are a real treat). Otherwise we pushed single beds together and placed Isabella on her sheepskin in the middle which worked well. If a room was carpeted, we made up her bed on the floor.

Isabella was drinking formula milk at that stage but organising bottles was no problem. Formula milk and bottled water were available everywhere we went and we quickly got into a routine for cleaning the associated equipment. I have also breastfed both children in developing countries, including Sri Lanka, and, if at all embarrassed, have flung a sarong over my shoulder; generally locals seem either disinterested or surprised to see a Western woman breast-feeding.

We found plenty of suitable food for kids – noodles, rice, milk rice, fruit, steamed or boiled vegetables, yoghurt, curd and bread. However, our infants generally lose their appetites in the tropics and unfamiliar territory. Friends carefully prepared plain fish and vegetable dishes for Isabella but she refused them, mainly wanting to drink. Sri Lankan curries tend to be very hot and spicy but some Western children love them. When I was a lecturer in Sri Lanka, a Western colleague's four-year-old daughter ate curries along with the rest of us and became more expert than us at eating with her hand in the local fashion.

The health risks in developing countries and the tropics is a real worry and it's worth taking preventative measures. Our children have all the required jabs and take an anti-malaria drug. We always buy bottled water for drinking and cleaning teeth. We try to put up a mosquito net over their beds and liberally apply mosquito repellent at dusk. We also rent more expensive rooms compared to when travelling solo, though in Sri Lanka a clean, bottom-end guest house can be fine and may offer the bonus of plenty of entertainment and company for your kids. Most Sri Lankan doctors speak English which is helpful and reassuring if you need to consult them, and there are decent hospitals in Colombo and Kandy.

Children in our experience suffer worse jet lag than adults; it's a real pain having to cope with their sleeplessness when you're tired yourself plus try to protect fellow hotel guests from their noise. As yet we haven't resorted to drugging the kids to get them to sleep after a long plane trip. There are homeopathic remedies for jet lag which may be worth trying. With small children we have simply pushed them around for hours in a stroller until they finally nod off. The problem compounds when you have a couple of children to deal with and you're travelling without a partner.

I have one unpleasant memory from our research trip to Sri Lanka. It was a Poya day, the full moon holiday, and we were at a playground in Kandy surrounded by hills dripping with tropical foliage; the full moon was rising. Isabella was dressed in white and playing happily on a merry-go-round; momentarily I glanced away to take in the view. Meanwhile a local man had seated his child next to Isabella and began whizzing them around quite fast. Isabella became dizzy and fell face down on the ground; she struggled to her feet, blood pouring from her dirt-filled mouth. She also had various cuts to her face. I had to carry her screaming to the nearest shop selling bottled water as she was so distressed by the dirt and grit in her mouth that nothing would placate her until her mouth was cleaned out. It was very dramatic at the time, but the wounds healed fairly quickly, although they may not have done so on the more humid coast. Although this incident could have happened anywhere, playgrounds in Sri Lanka are not as safe as at home and one needs to be vigilant.

Sri Lanka helped me to enjoy my pregnancy. I was purposeful with work to complete, surrounded by exotic scenery and infused with warmth. I kept my weight down, swam a lot, walked a lot and had plenty of company. Despite the difficulties of looking after Isabella on my own for much of the trip, I look back on it as a happy and relaxed time.

Susan Forsyth

JAVA

Peter & Lorraine Turner travelled through Java when Ruby (pictured with friend) was 2 ½ and Madeleine was three months in utero.

A FTER MANY, CHILDLESS TRIPS THROUGH INDONESIA I was looking forward to travelling with my family. Indonesians ask visitors a multitude of personal questions and high on the list are 'Are you married?' and 'How many children do you have?'. Unmarried, childless adults are pitied, and to choose to be so is considered strange. Travelling with my wife, Lorraine, and daughter, Ruby, gave me a status of normalcy I had never previously enjoyed in Indonesia.

We flew into Jakarta, the first stop on what was initially supposed to be a six-month trip through Java. The idea was that we would rent a house somewhere, probably in Yogyakarta, and use that as a base. Our plans were thrown up in the air when Lorraine found out she was pregnant just before departure.

Health suddenly became a major concern. We had weighed up all the pros and cons of travel with Ruby in often unhygienic Indonesia, but now there were extra concerns with Lorraine's health and that of our unborn child. Live vaccinations were out and it was very difficult to get reliable information about malaria. As we later found out, isolated outbreaks of malaria do occur in Java but it is virtually unheard of in the major cities and tourist areas. Neither Lorraine nor Ruby could take the latest, most effective anti-malarials so we relied on the first line of defence – mosquito repellent in the evenings and clothing that covered arms and legs. In the event of serious illness, I knew Jakarta had some excellent hospitals, otherwise Singapore or Darwin hospitals were only a few hours' flight away.

Jakarta is probably not the best city to introduce your children to Third World travel. It is noisy, crowded, disorienting and very hot. Yet despite some initial discomfort with the heat, Ruby took it in her stride. We visited all of Jakarta's

travel stories

family attractions: Taman Mini (an all-Indonesia theme park), Ragunan Zoo, and Fantasy World, undoubtedly the highlight for Ruby. Fantasy World is a Disneyland clone and Ruby sat enthralled through the 'small world' ride with its puppets of children from Indonesia and the world in national costume.

Ruby was treated like a superstar in Java. All children are idolised in Indonesia, but cute, foreign children, especially a 2½-year-old with red hair and blue eyes, was guaranteed flocks of admirers. People would come up and stroke her arm or hair and coo *'cantik'* (beautiful) or *'lucu'* (cute). At first Ruby loved the attention but then grew increasingly tired of it all. She would pull away and scowl at unwanted admirers – narrowing her eyes, dropping her brow and jutting out her chin in a ugly expression reminiscent of prehistoric Java Man.

From Jakarta we headed up into the hills to Bogor. This was to be Ruby's first real travelling test. We caught a *bajaj* (motorised three-wheeler) from Jalan Jaksa to Gambir station, then took the express train to Bogor, which was surprisingly comfortable and efficient. Travelling with Ruby turned out to be a breeze – after the first 15 minutes of any journey she would fall asleep and then wake up refreshed at the other end.

> **' We emerged at Bogor station, Ruby still asleep in Lorraine's arms, and me carrying all the luggage like a pack horse. '**

We emerged at Bogor station, Ruby still asleep in Lorraine's arms, and me carrying all the luggage like a pack horse. I started haggling with a trishaw driver outside the station when along came a tout from the hotel we wanted to stay at. We followed him, to a waiting car I thought, but he led us through a park to the main street and the public minibuses. We all crammed in for the short trip and finally unloaded at the other end. Ruby awoke, jumping up and down on the bed wanting to play, just as we sat down to relax and sip our customary welcome cup of coffee.

Bogor was certainly cooler and less crowded than Jakarta. We visited Bogor's famous botanic gardens, Ruby astride my shoulders almost the whole way around its 80 hectares. By now Ruby refused to walk, not only because of the heat but also because on my shoulders she was above the crowd and away from fussing bystanders. I began to develop the neck muscles of a rugby player, and soon learnt that carrying a child in the tropics was very hot work and to take taxis or trishaws whenever possible.

From Bogor we decided to go to Bandung then Pangandaran and make it our base for a few weeks. Pangandaran is an easygoing, overgrown fishing village turned beach resort, and a welcome break from the crowded cities of Java. Getting there was easy because of Java's excellent luxury minibuses that operate between the main cities, picking up and dropping off at hotels. We always tried to book the back row – three seats across with plenty of room for Ruby to stretch out and sleep.

Pangandaran's peak tourist season was still a couple of months away, so it was easy to negotiate a good deal for a longer stay. We found a delightful guest house with just a few bungalows, a swimming pool and luxuriant gardens right opposite a quiet stretch of beach. We rented bicycles with a child seat and Ruby was in heaven (and so was I, not having to carry her everywhere). Life for Ruby was a dip in the pool, a visit to her innumerable 'friends' around town and every afternoon she would shadow the old gardener who potted about the guest house. One day he picked all the flowers from a hibiscus bush just for Ruby because they were her favourites. Within two days the bush was a mass of flowers again.

> **' ...suddenly the cook ran out with Ruby sitting on his shoulders. Both giggled wildly as he ran around the restaurant before disappearing back into the kitchen. '**

As usual everyone fussed over Ruby and she soon became well known around town. In restaurants she would be whisked away by waitresses wanting to play with her or to show her off to friends down the street. One day after Ruby had disappeared out the back Lorraine started getting nervous, when suddenly the cook ran out with Ruby sitting on his shoulders. Both giggled wildly as he ran around the restaurant before disappearing back into the kitchen.

We made sure that Ruby always drank plenty of 'safe' liquids and avoided lengthy periods in the sun. Despite initial concerns about health, nothing had gone wrong apart from a few inevitable bouts of diarrhoea. In some ways it was a blessing in disguise, because Ruby loved the Asian squat toilets and was soon out of nappies altogether.

From Pangandaran we wanted to head through to Yogyakarta, but I didn't fancy the popular ferry ride to Cilacap. I was worried Ruby would find it as boring as I did on a previous visit and would throw a tantrum not long after leaving shore. Instead we decided to hire a car and driver (self-drive cars are only for the brave or foolish on Java's hectic roads), and visit Borobudur and Dieng Plateau as well as some off-the-beaten track destinations en route to

Yogyakarta. It was a great trip, though hectic, and Lorraine, now visibly pregnant, began to tire easily.

A hire car is certainly a great way to see Java if you can afford it. Through a budget tour operator, an air-conditioned Mitsubishi Colt minibus cost us US$35 per day, including driver but excluding petrol, and we also paid for the driver's hotel room each night.

Yogya was to be our next base for a few weeks. Yogya is the centre for Javanese culture and has plenty of attractions and amenities. The greatest attraction of Yogya for Ruby was the trishaws, which are everywhere and a fun way to travel around town.

It turned out to be very difficult to rent a house for only one or two months, but Yogya is a great place for reasonably priced accommodation and we found an old-fashioned family guest house. Our room had a huge carved bed that Ruby loved to jump on but one night she jumped on the edge and fell head-first on to the tiled floor. She cried and grabbed her shoulder, and throughout the night she kept waking up in pain.

The next morning we took her to the hospital. We were ushered into the emergency room, where a doctor ordered an X-ray straight away. The worst was confirmed – Ruby's collar bone was broken. She was given a bandage under the arms and around the neck and we were told there was nothing to do but wait – it should heal in about three weeks. The diagnosis proved to be correct, and though I wouldn't want to be in Java with a major illness, we were generally impressed with our only experience of Indonesian hospitals.

After much deliberation, we decided it was best if Lorraine and Ruby went home. Ruby soon healed but our increasing concern about the possibility of Lorraine getting sick tipped the balance. We would just have to come back to Indonesia – with two children next time.

Peter Turner

THAILAND

Kate Cody (pictured with Jackson) & Ben Taylor travelled to Thailand when Jackson was 20 months old & Lola was 2 months in utero.

W HEN WE WERE OFFERED TWO WEEKS in a suite of a luxury hotel in Hua Hin, Thailand, I had no problem abandoning my backpacker principals. Besides, I could always argue that travelling with our twenty-month-old son, Jackson, and the fact that I was eight-weeks-pregnant meant we had to go upmarket.

I was again experiencing the phenomena of morning sickness all day long. At home I had been unable to cook because the smell of frying garlic or onion made me feel sick. It was a joy to eat delicious *phat thai* or *tom yam kung*: fried noodles and hot and sour prawn soup that had been prepared by someone else spared me the nausea. Too bad if the baby was born a chilli addict.

Morning and afternoon I laid by the pool reading while Ben and Jackson played on the Hua Hin beach or splashed in the babies' pool nearby. Our day was breakfast, pool, lunch, nap, beach, dinner. No museums, palaces, temples or art galleries. More blissful inactivity than I had experienced since Jackson's birth.

Some days we went to a nearby Raffles-style hotel, Sofitel, to drink English tea and to see the baby elephant they kept there to entertain the guests at the poolside. Although the elephant was only waist high to an adult it towered over Jackson, but he wasn't scared. It was me who felt uncomfortable when it began frisking me with the end of its trunk in a desperate attempt to find the bananas I had stowed in my backpack.

Jackson was just beginning to talk so we taught him how to say '*sawat-dii khrap*' to greet people. He made a lot of friends and whenever we were within the hotel grounds there was always someone ready to entertain him. He fed broken biscuits to the mammoth carp in the ornamental ponds or ate sweets and nuts with the elegant women who worked in the cocktail bar. He arranged matchbox car rallies with the marketing manager and typed on his shy assistant's computer. Everywhere we went people called out 'Jackson'.

We bought huge bags of pomelo, mangosteen, longan and rambutans to keep in our room, reasoning that Jackson could survive on long-life cow's milk and fruit if need be. Jackson feasted his way through the range of Thai fruit; an invasion of ants ate their way through the discarded skins.

At night we would go into the nearby town and eat spicy noodles and banana fritters at one of the market stalls. Jackson wolfed down everything and only once came to grief when he ate a whole chilli with his fried morning glory. 'More' became another of his new words. His appetite and his sturdy toddler body was much admired.

A couple of times we ate at one of the seafood restaurants that were elevated on stilts over the beach and the town's sewerage outlet. Jackson stayed at the table just long enough for a mouthful of crab, rice or *plaa lard phrik* (fried chilli fish), before being taken off to play hide and seek with the children whose mothers ran the restaurant. If there were no kids to play with he would happily follow the numerous mangy cats that hung around. It was impossible to stop him from touching them. He had a repertoire of animal noises and as far as he knew that furry thing that said 'miaow' was there to pat.

Geckos are a common enough sight in most parts of the world and they always find their way into your room. But we gained a new appreciation for them in Thailand when 'gecko' was added to Jackson's rapidly expanding vocabulary, and because they provided the simplest entertainment in our non-descript hotel room. We would spot that unmistakable shape and translucent flesh against the wall or ceiling: the lizard, still at first, then skipping across the wall or ceiling. And if Jackson couldn't find a gecko we had to draw them for him, a request that continued for months and led to many chalk drawings on the cement paths of our Melbourne garden.

Katie Cody

TURKEY

**Ruth Armes &
Rod Gibson
travelled to
Eastern Turkey
when Rupert
(pictured) was 10
months old.**

BEFORE HAVING RUPERT, OUR FIRST BABY, we had done a fair amount of backpacking. When he was three-months-old we ventured forth again. Being unsure of ourselves we hired a car and went to southern Spain. Having deluded ourselves that we were near to home and quite safe we lost all our luggage and had to drive hundreds of km through the mountains without a side window. Despite our shortlived misery we had determined that travelling with a baby was feasible.

With Rupert now 10-months-old we arrived in Istanbul; simultaneously our luggage arrived in Portugal. We were travelling with one backpack between the three of us, plus a baby carrier. Fortunately we had several nappies in our daypack, and past experience of no luggage, so the three days it took our backpack to find us passed relatively calmly.

Our pack was mostly taken up with baby maintenance equipment. We had planned to use cloth nappies, but it was possible to buy disposable nappies in Turkey.

Rupert mostly relied on breast milk for nourishment, though we had a spirit stove with which to cook the occasional meal for him. It also provided us with tea and coffee. This proved essential as sitting in cafes with a bored crawling infant can leave you more stressed than when you went in. Ruth often discreetly breastfed Rupert in public places such as buses and she never experienced any embarrassment or difficulty. For restaurant meals we had a clamp-on seat that proved very successful, though our choice of restaurant was often determined by whether they had the right sort of tables.

We had decided that Rupert would soon get bored with any toys we took, so we just hoped he would improvise. This I think proved the right decision, though we had to put up with him rifling the pack to find something new to play with.

Rupert was at the stage that whenever anybody smiled at him he beamed back. As he rode on my back he drew a lot of attention. After three days in Istanbul he became well known and somehow earned the name 'Agoo'. Wherever we went the street traders waved and shouted out 'Baby, baby, Agoo' to earn themselves a Rupert smile. In return he received many gifts.

Rupert had always slept in our beds at home, so sleeping arrangements whilst we were away was not a problem. On arriving at a new hotel room I always do a safety check and on three occasions now I have found live wires were a child could reach them. For parents of a toddler, window catches and the temperature of the hot water tap are also worth checking.

On the fourth day we got the last seats on an internal flight to Erzurum, two thirds of the way east. The remainder of the journey out to Dogubeyazit we did by coach. This proved a bit of a nightmare as Rupert refused to settle and left us frazzled after a four-hour wrestling match.

> *Rupert had fallen asleep in their car so we put him in an ante room and they posted a guard to come and tell us when he woke up.*

Dogubeyazit itself was a success. Mount Ararat should be on every traveller's itinerary. We spent several pleasant days walking in the hills. From here, we made the journey south to Van along the little used road through Galdiran in a much overcrowded and dilapidated *dolmus*. Again Rupert proved very troublesome, but nevertheless the journey was fascinating. On the boat trip back from the Armenian church Akdamar Kilisesi, situated on an island on Lake Van, we met a group of army officers who invited us back to the base for lunch and drinks. Rupert had fallen asleep in their car so we put him in an ante room and they posted a guard to come and tell us when he woke up.

By now we were 1700 km from Istanbul and were becoming anxious about bus journeys. We tried booking a flight west again but nothing was available for months. It then occurred to us that if we caught night buses Rupert would sleep through the journey. This strategy worked really well. It often meant arriving at our destination in the early hours of the morning, but Rupert would usually sleep through the transfer.

Our next memorable event was Nemrut Dagi, near Malatya. We had to do the journey up the mountain during the day. Seeing the colossal heads, spectac-

travel stories

ular and eerie, looking over the surrounding desert landscape was a worthwhile experience, but during the night Rupert decided to cut a molar, the hotel's electricity failed, our torch broke and there was no moon. We slept little and Rupert cried a lot! Our misery was more than offset though when we reached the bottom the next day. The Malatya region's Sub-governor's ten year old son Cha Chin had been in the booking office when we booked the trip up. Being much entertained by Rupert, and knowing the guide well, he had come on the trip. Somehow he had sent a message ahead, for when we returned to Malatya our party was whisked off to the Sub-governor' residence outside of town to be fed bowls of cherries and tea whilst children in traditional costumes danced for our benefit. The Sub-governor gave a speech saying it was in honour of Rupert being the youngest person to ascend Nemrut Dagi and Ruth was presented with a large bouquet of flowers whilst official photographs were taken.

That night we caught the night bus out to Cappadocia. Exploring the underground cities there, though fun, proved arduous because of the low ceilings. With Rupert on my back I often had to crawl along the passageways.

> *They insisted that we join their picnic which consisted of three generations of the female line of three families.*

Our next stop was Bursa, right back in the west and just a few hours from Istanbul. After bathing in the hot spring water we took the cable car up to Uludag. At the top we met four young teenage girls who wanted to practise their English on us. They insisted that we join their picnic which consisted of three generations of the female line of three families. The girls chatted, the mothers, who spoke no English, plied us with food and the grandmothers fretted about Rupert getting cold. We had met a lot of concern throughout the county about Rupert being cold. Rupert, coming from England, was used to it being a lot colder, whereas the Turks swaddle their babies in blankets to the point where we worried about them overheating.

We made the final leg of the journey back to Istanbul by bus and ferry. On arrival at the airport a disagreeable airline representative informed us that we didn't have seats on the plane, and from then on he refused to talk to us. After much argument and pleading with other officials, and no doubt helped by the presence of Rupert, we finally boarded a plane to London. On returning home Rupert seemed most bemused that people in the street kept ignoring him, despite his best smiles.

Rod Gibson

INDEX

PLANET TALK

Lonely Planet's FREE quarterly newsletter

We love hearing from you and think you'd like to hear from us.

When...is the right time to see reindeer in Finland?
Where...can you hear the best palm-wine music in Ghana?
How...do you get from Asunción to Areguá by steam train?
What...is the best way to see India?

For the answer to these and many other questions read PLANET TALK.

Every issue is packed with up-to-date travel news and advice including:

- a letter from Lonely Planet co-founders Tony and Maureen Wheeler
- go behind the scenes on the road with a Lonely Planet author
- feature article on an important and topical travel issue
- a selection of recent letters from travellers
- details on forthcoming Lonely Planet promotions
- complete list of Lonely Planet products

To join our mailing list contact any Lonely Planet office.

Also available: Lonely Planet T-shirts. 100% heavyweight cotton.

LONELY PLANET ONLINE

Get the latest travel information before you leave or while you're on the road

Whether you've just begun planning your next trip, or you're chasing down specific info on currency regulations or visa requirements, check out Lonely Planet Online for up-to-the minute travel information.

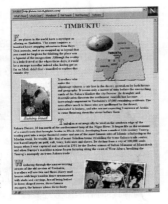

As well as travel profiles of your favourite destinations (including maps and photos), you'll find current reports from our researchers and other travellers, updates on health and visas, travel advisories, and discussion of the ecological and political issues you need to be aware of as you travel.

There's also an online travellers' forum where you can share your experience of life on the road, meet travel companions and ask other travellers for their recommendations and advice. We also have plenty of links to other online sites useful to independent travellers.

And of course we have a complete and up-to-date list of all Lonely Planet travel products including guides, phrasebooks, atlases, Journeys and videos and a simple online ordering facility if you can't find the book you want elsewhere.

www.lonelyplanet.com
or
AOL keyword: lp

LONELY PLANET PRODUCTS

Lonely Planet is known worldwide for publishing practical, reliable and no-nonsense travel information in our guides and on our web site. The Lonely Planet list covers just about every accessible part of the world. Currently there are nine series: *travel guides*, *shoestring guides*, *walking guides*, *city guides*, *phrasebooks*, *audio packs*, *travel atlases*, *Journeys* – a unique collection of travel writing and *Pisces Books* - diving and snorkeling guides.

EUROPE

Amsterdam • Austria • Baltic States phrasebook • Berlin • Britain • Canary Islands• Central Europe on a shoestring • Central Europe phrasebook • Czech & Slovak Republics • Denmark • Dublin • Eastern Europe on a shoestring • Eastern Europe phrasebook • Estonia, Latvia & Lithuania • Finland • France • French phrasebook • Germany • German phrasebook • Greece • Greek phrasebook • Hungary • Iceland, Greenland & the Faroe Islands • Ireland • Italian phrasebook • Italy • Lisbon • London • Mediterranean Europe on a shoestring • Mediterranean Europe phrasebook • Paris • Poland • Portugal • Portugal travel atlas • Prague • Romania & Moldova • Russia, Ukraine & Belarus • Russian phrasebook • Scandinavian & Baltic Europe on a shoestring • Scandinavian Europe phrasebook • Slovenia • Spain • Spanish phrasebook • St Petersburg • Switzerland •Trekking in Spain • Ukrainian phrasebook • Vienna • Walking in Britain • Walking in Italy • Walking in Switzerland • Western Europe on a shoestring • Western Europe phrasebook

Travel Literature: The Olive Grove: Travels in Greece

NORTH AMERICA

Alaska • Backpacking in Alaska • Baja California • California & Nevada • Canada • Chicago • Deep South• Florida • Hawaii • Honolulu • Los Angeles • Mexico • Mexico City • Miami • New England • New Orleans • New York City • New York, New Jersey & Pennsylvania • Pacific Northwest USA • Rocky Mountain States • San Francisco • Southwest USA • USA phrasebook • Washington, DC & the Capital Region

Travel Literature: Drive thru America

CENTRAL AMERICA & THE CARIBBEAN

•Bahamas and Turks & Caicos •Bermuda •Central America on a shoestring • Costa Rica • Cuba •Eastern Caribbean •Guatemala, Belize & Yucatán: La Ruta Maya • Jamaica

SOUTH AMERICA

Argentina, Uruguay & Paraguay • Bolivia • Brazil • Brazilian phrasebook • Buenos Aires • Chile & Easter Island • Chile & Easter Island travel atlas • Colombia Ecuador & the Galápagos Islands • Latin American Spanish phrasebook • Peru • Quechua phrasebook • Rio de Janeiro • South America on a shoestring • Trekking in the Patagonian Andes • Venezuela

Travel Literature: Full Circle: A South American Journey

ISLANDS OF THE INDIAN OCEAN

Madagascar & Comoros • Maldives• Mauritius, Réunion & Seychelles

AFRICA

Africa - the South • Africa on a shoestring • Arabic (Moroccan) phrasebook • Cairo • Cape Town • Central Africa • East Africa • Egypt • Egypt travel atlas• Ethiopian (Amharic) phrasebook • Kenya • Kenya travel atlas • Malawi, Mozambique & Zambia • Morocco • North Africa • South Africa, Lesotho & Swaziland • South Africa, Lesotho & Swaziland travel atlas • Swahili phrasebook • Tunisia • Trekking in East Africa • West Africa • Zimbabwe, Botswana & Namibia • Zimbabwe, Botswana & Namibia travel atlas

Travel Literature: The Rainbird: A Central African Journey • Songs to an African Sunset: A Zimbabwean Story

MAIL ORDER

Lonely Planet products are distributed worldwide. They are also available by mail order from Lonely Planet, so if you have difficulty finding a title please write to us. North American and South American residents should write to 150 Linden St, Oakland CA 94607, USA; European and African residents should write to 10a Spring Place, London NW5 3BH; and residents of other countries to PO Box 617, Hawthorn, Victoria 3122, Australia.

NORTH-EAST ASIA

Beijing • Cantonese phrasebook • China • Hong Kong • Hong Kong, Macau & Guangzhou • Japan • Japanese phrasebook • Japanese audio pack • Korea • Korean phrasebook • Mandarin phrasebook • Mongolia • Mongolian phrasebook • North-East Asia on a shoestring • Seoul • Taiwan • Tibet • Tibet phrasebook • Tokyo

Travel Literature: Lost Japan

MIDDLE EAST & CENTRAL ASIA

Arab Gulf States • Arabic (Egyptian) phrasebook • Central Asia • Central Asia phrasebook • Iran • Israel & the Palestinian Territories • Israel & the Palestinian Territories travel atlas • Istanbul • Jerusalem • Jordan & Syria • Jordan, Syria & Lebanon travel atlas • Lebanon • Middle East • Turkey • Turkish phrasebook • Turkey travel atlas • Yemen

Travel Literature: The Gates of Damascus • Kingdom of the Film Stars: Journey into Jordan

ALSO AVAILABLE:

Brief Encounters • Travel with Children • Traveller's Tales

INDIAN SUBCONTINENT

Bangladesh • Bengali phrasebook • Delhi • Goa • Hindi/Urdu phrasebook • India • India & Bangladesh travel atlas • Indian Himalaya • Karakoram Highway • Nepal • Nepali phrasebook • Pakistan • Rajasthan • Sri Lanka • Sri Lanka phrasebook • Trekking in the Indian Himalaya • Trekking in the Karakoram & Hindukush • Trekking in the Nepal Himalaya

Travel Literature: In Rajasthan • Shopping for Buddhas

SOUTH-EAST ASIA

Bali & Lombok • Bangkok • Burmese phrasebook • Cambodia • Ho Chi Minh City • Indonesia • Indonesian phrasebook • Indonesian audio pack • Jakarta • Java • Laos • Lao phrasebook • Laos travel atlas • Malay phrasebook • Malaysia, Singapore & Brunei • Myanmar (Burma) • Philippines • Pilipino phrasebook • Singapore • South-East Asia on a shoestring • South-East Asia phrasebook • Thailand • Thailand's Islands & Beaches • Thailand travel atlas • Thai phrasebook • Thai audio pack • Thai Hill Tribes phrasebook • Vietnam • Vietnamese phrasebook • Vietnam travel atlas

AUSTRALIA & THE PACIFIC

Australia • Australian phrasebook • Bushwalking in Australia • Bushwalking in Papua New Guinea • Fiji • Fijian phrasebook • Islands of Australia's Great Barrier Reef • Melbourne • Micronesia • New Caledonia • New South Wales • New Zealand • Northern Territory • Outback Australia • Papua New Guinea • Papua New Guinea phrasebook • Queensland • Rarotonga & the Cook Islands • Samoa • Solomon Islands • South Australia • Sydney • Tahiti & French Polynesia • Tasmania • Tonga • Tramping in New Zealand • Vanuatu • Victoria • Western Australia

Travel Literature: Islands in the Clouds • Sean & David's Long Drive

ANTARCTICA

Antarctica

THE LONELY PLANET STORY

Lonely Planet published its first book in 1973 in response to the numerous 'How did you do it?' questions Maureen and Tony Wheeler were asked after driving, bussing, hitching, sailing and railing their way from England to Australia.

Written at a kitchen table and hand collated, trimmed and stapled, *Across Asia on the Cheap* became an instant local bestseller, inspiring thoughts of another book.

Eighteen months in South-East Asia resulted in their second guide, *South-East Asia on a shoestring*, which they put together in a backstreet Chinese hotel in Singapore in 1975. The 'yellow bible', as it quickly became known to backpackers around the world, soon became *the* guide to the region. It has sold well over half a million copies and is now in its 9th edition, still retaining its familiar yellow cover.

Today there are over 350 titles, including travel guides, walking guides, language kits & phrasebooks, travel atlases and travel literature. The company is the largest independent travel publisher in the world. Although Lonely Planet initially specialised in guides to Asia, today there are few corners of the globe that have not been covered.

The emphasis continues to be on travel for independent travellers. Tony and Maureen still travel for several months of each year and play an active part in the writing, updating and quality control of Lonely Planet's guides.

They have been joined by over 80 authors and 200 staff at our offices in Melbourne (Australia), Oakland (USA), London (UK) and Paris (France). Travellers themselves also make a valuable contribution to the guides through the feedback we receive in thousands of letters each year and on our web site.

The people at Lonely Planet strongly believe that travellers can make a positive contribution to the countries they visit, both through their appreciation of the countries' culture, wildlife and natural features, and through the money they spend. In addition, the company makes a direct contribution to the countries and regions it covers. Since 1986 a percentage of the income from each book has been donated to ventures such as famine relief in Africa; aid projects in India; agricultural projects in Central America; Greenpeace's efforts to halt French nuclear testing in the Pacific; and Amnesty International.

'I hope we send people out with the right attitude about travel. You realise when you travel that there are so many different perspectives about the world, so we hope these books will make people more interested in what they see. Guidebooks can't really guide people. All you can do is point them in the right direction.'

– Tony Wheeler

LONELY PLANET PUBLICATIONS

Australia
PO Box 617, Hawthorn 3122, Victoria
tel: (03) 9819 1877 fax: (03) 9819 6459
e-mail: talk2us@lonelyplanet.com.au

USA
150 Linden St
Oakland, CA 94607
tel: (510) 893 8555 TOLL FREE: 800 275-8555
fax: (510) 893 8572
e-mail: info@lonelyplanet.com

UK
10a Spring Place,
London NW5 3BH
tel: (0171) 428 4800 fax: (0171) 428 4828
e-mail: go@lonelyplanet.co.uk

France:
71 bis rue du Cardinal Lemoine, 75005 Paris
tel: 01 44 32 06 20 fax: 01 46 34 72 55
e-mail: bip@lonelyplanet.fr

World Wide Web: http://www.lonelyplanet.com
or *AOL* keyword: lp